# The IRS—Our Government in Action

# The IRS—Our Government in Action

◆

## Don't Trust Them for Anything!

*Rick Meyer*

iUniverse, Inc.

New York  Lincoln  Shanghai

# The IRS—Our Government in Action
## Don't Trust Them for Anything!

iUniverse books may be ordered through booksellers or by contacting:

iUniverse
2021 Pine Lake Road, Suite 100
Lincoln, NE 68512
www.iuniverse.com
1-800-Authors (1-800-288-4677)

ISBN-13: 978-0-595-38752-6 (pbk)
ISBN-13: 978-0-595-83135-7 (ebk)
ISBN-10: 0-595-38752-7 (pbk)
ISBN-10: 0-595-83135-4 (ebk)

Printed in the United States of America

# Contents

PREFACE. . . . . . . . . . . . . . . . . . . . . . . . . . . . . . . . . . . . . . . . . ix

CHAPTER 1     The Early Years . . . . . . . . . . . . . . . . . . . . . . . . 1

CHAPTER 2     Into the Real World. . . . . . . . . . . . . . . . . . . . . 6

CHAPTER 3     The College Years . . . . . . . . . . . . . . . . . . . . 10

CHAPTER 4     Into The Industrial World. . . . . . . . . . . . . . . 12

CHAPTER 5     The Pathway to Problems . . . . . . . . . . . . . . . 21

CaptionEXHIBIT NO.1. . . . . . . . . . . . . . . . . . . . . . . . . . . . . 49

CaptionEXHIBIT NO. 2 . . . . . . . . . . . . . . . . . . . . . . . . . . . . 52

CaptionEXHIBIT No. 3. . . . . . . . . . . . . . . . . . . . . . . . . . . . . 54

CaptionEXHIBIT No. 4. . . . . . . . . . . . . . . . . . . . . . . . . . . . . 58

CaptionEXHIBIT NO. 5 . . . . . . . . . . . . . . . . . . . . . . . . . . . . 61

CaptionEXHIBIT No. 6. . . . . . . . . . . . . . . . . . . . . . . . . . . . . 63

CaptionEXHIBIT No. 7. . . . . . . . . . . . . . . . . . . . . . . . . . . . . 65

CaptionEXHIBIT No. 8. . . . . . . . . . . . . . . . . . . . . . . . . . . . . 67

CaptionEXHIBIT No. 9. . . . . . . . . . . . . . . . . . . . . . . . . . . . . 69

CaptionEXHIBIT NO. 10 . . . . . . . . . . . . . . . . . . . . . . . . . . . 71

CaptionEXHIBIT NO. 11 . . . . . . . . . . . . . . . . . . . . . . . . . . . 73

CaptionEXHIBIT NO. 12 . . . . . . . . . . . . . . . . . . . . . . . . . . . 79

CaptionEXHIBIT NO. 13 . . . . . . . . . . . . . . . . . . . . . . . . . . . 82

CaptionEXHIBIT NO. 14 .................................. 84

CaptionEXHIBIT NO. 15 .................................. 86

CaptionEXHIBIT NO. 16 .................................. 88

CaptionEXHIBIT NO. 17 .................................. 91

CaptionEXHIBIT NO. 18 .................................. 94

CaptionEXHIBIT NO. 19 .................................. 96

CaptionEXHIBIT NO. 20 .................................. 98

CaptionEXHIBIT NO. 21 .................................. 100

CaptionEXHIBIT NO. 22 .................................. 103

CaptionEXHIBIT NO. 23 .................................. 106

CaptionEXHIBIT No. 24 .................................. 109

CaptionEXHIBIT NO. 25 .................................. 111

CaptionEXHIBIT NO. 26 .................................. 114

CaptionEXHIBIT NO 27 .................................. 116

CaptionEXHIBIT NO 28 .................................. 118

CaptionEXHIBIT NO. 29 .................................. 121

CaptionEXHIBIT NO. 30 .................................. 125

CaptionEXHIBIT NO. 31 .................................. 127

CaptionEXHIBIT No. 32 .................................. 129

CaptionEXHIBIT No. 33 .................................. 131

CaptionEXHIBIT NO. 34 .................................. 133

CaptionEXHIBIT NO. 35 .................................. 136

CaptionEXHIBIT NO. 36 .................................. 142

CaptionEXHIBIT NO. 37 .................................. 145

CaptionEXHIBIT NO. 38 .................................. 150

CaptionEXHIBIT NO. 39 . . . . . . . . . . . . . . . . . . . . . . . . . . . . . . . .154

CaptionEXHIBIT NO. 40 . . . . . . . . . . . . . . . . . . . . . . . . . . . . . . . .156

# *PREFACE*

This is a story that has to be told. It is a record of the trials, harassment and personal depression one encounters when faced with a charge from the Internal Revenue Service.

Let me state-right up front-the Internal Revenue Service is due the monies which drive this entire pilgrimage. My argument has always been that I am not the party liable for the funds due. I believe I provide more than adequate substantiation of my argument with the numerous exhibits that are provided.

Although this book is presented as a fictional novel, the exhibits of Internal Revenue Service correspondence covering a fifteen year period indicates the reality that this writing and actual experience is very close to true life.

First of all, doesn't fifteen years seem as a quite lengthy period of time to be battling a government agency? My opposition, as indicated, is the Internal Revenue Service. I should mention that this agency reportedly does not appreciate being identified as the IRS. From this point forward, my opposition will be identified as the IRS.

Initially, I was very hesitant to write such a book which does not cast a very positive light on this agency. But, as you progress through the pages, eventually you will understand why this book had to be written. How much harassment, misleading information,unilateral actions without any response, threats and just plain old falsehoods must one endure?

I didn't write the book to indicate that I am totally innocent. I do bear some of the responsibility for the situation, and all that follows. However, it is written to make anyone and everyone aware of the issues, frustrations and total exasperation one must endure when pursued by the IRS.

To them it doesn't matter if you are the responsible party. If they have a name, extenuating conditions play no role. They put all their efforts into the path (party) of least resistance. This argument is evidenced early in the story when the company known as Florida Corp. acknowledges the liability of the company for past taxes due the IRS. They make only six of seventy legally responsible payments. Even though the IRS has total authority to seize assets for remaining payments, they take no action. Instead, they (IRS) continue their pursuit of me (Rick Meyer).

This book is primarily for present and future small business entrepreneurs. The purpose is to give you insight into what you can expect if you find yourself in a position where you must make a choice between paying for supplies or paying your obligation for payroll taxes. For those of you considering starting your own company, are you prepared to make such decisions? I have no straightforward answer for you, but these are issues you must consider. The text and Exhibits can prove to be quite technical in nature. I apologize, but I want to provide you with actual examples of the type of correspondence you would be receiving from the IRS.

There are many other individuals who may gain worthwhile insight into the internal workings of government enforcement agencies. Business students, tax accountants and lawyers might all benefit from this story of personal emotion, frustration and total lack of any type of formal procedures being utilized in such situations by the IRS. The IRS controls all aspects of the event. You can only respond, you can never initiate any action.

Finally, anyone interested in reading the saga of 'a plain old Joe' who grows up with his dreams and desires. One day he has the opportunity to realize this dream. He knows he is not in the best financial condition to pursue this effort, but 'hey, this is what I always wanted', and he makes the move.

There are many highs and lows throughout this story. Overall, my life has been very good. The 'downs' were primarily of my own doing. I accept that.

The story begins with my childhood and my family. Growing up in a small town in eastern Pennsylvania. We didn't have any extras, but we had what we needed. My father died at a very young age. At the time of his death the children ranged in age from 4–19. There were six children. Five of the six earned college degrees, and we all went our own way into life.

I was probably the most aggressive, relative to my goals in life. I always sought 'financial independence'. Not a life of luxury, just a financial condition that permitted some of the extras we never had as children.

In today's economy, and in retirement, a net tax income of $55,000/year would suffice.

I have held many excellent positions and have really enjoyed life. I had always wanted my own company (metals related) and in the late 1980's the opportunity presented itself, and I went after it.

The subject that hangs in my craw is that I wasn't more cynical when dealing with people who would indirectly effect/control a major portion of my adult life. When my financial situation began to fall apart, I had to give up sole ownership of the company. At that point I decided to leave the company. My letter of resignation stipulated that in return for giving up my twenty percent ownership in the company, the company would accept all liabilities against the company. My conditions were accepted, but it was a year or two later that I learned that the company was not held to these liabilities. This is the major point I have never been able to accept.

To me, it is a case of the IRS viewing it as much easier to come after me, as an individual, than to go after a corporation. This whole issue stinks to high heaven on the side of both the IRS and the corporation. However, I must give the corporation credit. They were able to scam the IRS and leave me holding the bag. More power to them!

From 1992 to the present time, the issue remains open. During this time my age goes from 55 to 68. My industry of expertise (iron and steel) is extremely consolidated, which results in much less employment opportunities. My wife and I also own a well known local restaurant in our home area. The restaurant is located in a medium sized city which is suffering from the demographic changes experienced by most cities. We always had a very good business, but by the mid-nineties sales started to fall and several customers mentioned that they regretted to tell us, but they wouldn't be coming back. They feared the possibility of violence, even though we never had any such problems.

In the late nineties we filed for bankruptcy. We shut the restaurant. I couldn't find any employment paying more than $12.00/hour. I had the IRS problems hanging over me, credit card debt from the Florida company exceeded $150,000 and I was now earning a very minimal wage.

In 2003 I retired. Actually, I didn't really retire. I had an opportunity to earn some really good money, so I terminated my employment at that time. This opportunity didn't last too long, so in reality, I did retire at that time. Within three months I was looking for a part time job. I need a reason to get up every morning. I don't like the fact that every day is the weekend. I have always been someone who liked the challenge of seeking a goal, more than savoring the rewards after achieving the goal. I like the chase more than the reward.

To me, reaching retirement is a goal. Now that I have reached that goal, what do I do now? Play golf every day, run six miles every day, fish, work in the yard, travel? These are things I enjoy doing, in between real responsibilities. My best opportunity was to become an adjunct professor at a local community college. It was located about 60 miles from my home. I then saw an advertisement for a technician for a local metals company. I called, interviewed, and got the job.

A new job. Things are going very well. All of a sudden I get-a lien on our home, a frozen bank account, wage garnishment. You seek answers, you get no response from the IRS. They take what they want, and you adjust.

Approximately twelve months later, I again seek some answers. I am told, by letter, that the garnishment will continue for two more years. No matter what happens there will be no more legal action against me. Two months later I receive a notice telling me that the IRS is considering taking a significant portion of my social security benefits.

By late 2005, I think I can see the end in 2008. Will I be capable of maintaining full time employment? Will my wife and I have sufficient income to live above the poverty level? Will we have a life? Who knows?

I hope you enjoy the story. I am certain everyone who reads this novel will have definite opinions as to what I should have done differently, but for me, it is over. I have moved on and hope for the best.

Rick Meyer

# 1

## *The Early Years*

I was born in Sept of 1937, the second of six children, to Verna and Paul Meyer. Our home was in a small town of 2500 in the mid Atlantic region.. Our first home was a frame rental property. Inhabitants included not only my family, but several rodents who did remain in the basement. I hate rats. We also had an out-house. We used it during the day, and a enclosed container at night. In the morning one of my brothers, or I, would take it out and dump it into the hole in the outhouse. The outhouse had two seats, but I don't ever recall anyone else being inside with me. I am sure that at some time when there was a real emergency, one of my brothers joined me.

My mother never worked after beginning a family, until later in life. My father worked in the local steel mill. Life was more or less routine. Early in our lives our father started raising rabbits for sale, in order to supplement his income. I vividly recall the assignment for my brothers and I to fill the water bowls and feed dishes each day. Both dishes were made of cast iron, and in the winter time we had to break and remove the ice from the water dish before we could add fresh water. I also recall climbing on top of the rabbit hutches, I estimate they were 6–8 feet high, and jumping from them, pretending to be Superman.

Christmas time was always the highlight of the year. As I look back, I am truly amazed that we received such nice gifts. When you reached the fourth grade, you got a new bicycle for Christmas. When I finally got mine, I took it with me to our grandparents' home and spent the entire day riding it on the adjacent street. Near the end of the day, I started to feel a pain on the inside of my thighs, but I just kept riding. When we got home that evening and I took off my trousers, prior to bed, I noticed that my whole groin area was rubbed raw. It didn't really matter, I enjoyed the ride.

After my second brother, came two sisters. At this time my parents bought a home closer to my father's job. They had purchased a building lot a few years earlier with the intent to build. However, I assume they felt buying one was a better deal for them. It was a row home, and it was great. Indoor plumbing and separate beds for each of us children. My two brothers and I slept on the third floor. My older brother in one room, and my other brother and I in another room. There was no heat on the third floor, but lots of blankets.

Life continued, and at age 10 or 11 we each started delivering the daily newspaper. At one point the three of us delivered essentially all the newspapers in our town. This included morning and evening edition. We could sit down and name almost ever family in town, street by street, and also tell you the daily edition delivered to each home. We knew this, because every Saturday we had to go to each customer and collect the money due for the week's delivery. Most homes had a pretty good smell, especially on Saturday when most mothers were baking. I suppose that at this point the evidence that I was different than my brother's began to emerge. This information was only uncovered within the past year. Example: We had to walk almost one mile to the newspaper stand to pick up the newspapers for delivery. At 5:00 A.M. in the morning, in the winter, it is dark at this time of day. My one brother recently mentioned that when he walked the street, he stayed near to the buildings so that he would not be noticeable to anyone looking to harm someone. My other brother said he walked in the middle of the pavement so he had ample opportunity to run either way if someone same upon him. I mentioned that I walked up the alleys, looking for cigarette butts to light up and smoke on my way to the news stand.

During this same period, I joined the Cub Scouts. My mother was Den Mother and several of my school friends also joined. We met at my house, and used the garage for the meetings. In the winter time I put an electric radiator in the garage several hours before the meeting, but it was still very cold at meeting time. I don't remember being cold, we had a brief meeting and everyone went home. I liked the uniforms, navy blue with gold trim.

Throughout the years my brothers and I enjoyed the atmosphere of small town USA. There was a ball field at the community park, but it was about one mile from our home. All of the neighborhood boys would go to a nearby field, and make our own ball diamond. There were rocks everywhere. We used baseballs that were completely covered with 'tire' tape so that we could continue to use them. They must have weighed three times the regulation weight. You could not hit to right field. That was because it was a very steep hill. When the ball hit there, it would immediately roll down the hill and the batter had a home run. In left field you had a home run if the baseball cleared the tree line. These trees were about 15 feet high, but it was only about 100 feet from home base.

You normally also had a home run if you hit the ball through the tree line. By the time the outfielder went through the trees, recovered the ball and threw it home, you were around the bases.

I recall that many times as I stood in the outfield I wished we had a better field, uniforms and good equipment Today, in hindsight, I believe the conditions, atmosphere and camaraderie gave us a better base for the future than the well managed and controlled conditions so prevalent in the lives of young people nowadays. If we wanted something, we had to get it, or make it. These conditions also developed leadership skills. We all had our strengths and weaknesses. Everyone recognized who was best in what areas. Guidance for the group came through a combination of physical strength, intelligence and wit. And, we all accepted it. In today's world children have no opportunity to engage in any of those mechanisms. Everything is organized, planned and controlled for them.

We continued with the newspaper routes, I mainly went swimming in the summer months while my brothers, Ken and Gordon, played baseball.

Around the age of twelve I joined the Boy Scouts. I really enjoyed this activity. We camped, hiked, learned basic survival skills and just did many interesting things. Again, my closest friends also belonged. Will, Don and Warren were my best friends both in and out of school. We all belonged to the same Scout patrol.

Around this same time I also joined a community baseball league. I started in center field. Because I was left handed, they also made me a pitcher. I remember in one game I hit two home runs. The first was between center and left field (I batted right handed. This is probably the reason I was really not very good in baseball, or golf). The second was a long high hit to left field. One of my neighbor friends was playing left field. He came running in to catch the ball, and it went over his head.

Those were really good times. As we entered what is now known as senior high (9th through 12th), my interests started to separate from Ken and Gordon. They continued in baseball and basketball and soccer. I liked soccer, but again I really wasn't that good. There are two episodes worth mentioning. Since I was left-handed the coach thought I kicked with my left foot so he made me a left halfback. In one game the opponent kicked a ball to the goal from the right hand side of the field. When the goalie went out for the ball to the right, I had to play in front of the goal. The ball soared over the goalie's head and came right for me. I put up my right leg to deflect the ball away from the goal. Regrettably, the ball just grazed my leg and went into the goal. The next day the newspaper reported our win, but stated in the scoring. Meyer, Belmont, scored for Fleetside. Note: Our goalie was the same neighbor who ran under my hit in the baseball game that gave me a home run. In another game against my future wife's school I was again playing halfback and a ball came to me. My job was to kick the ball over the heads of our linemen so they could drive to the opponents goal. I kicked a little too hard. The ball went over our linemen, over their linemen, halfbacks and fullbacks and into the goal. This was from mid field. In reality, I really wasn't much of a player.

While in the 10th grade, our homeroom teacher asked me, Will and another student to remain after the dismissal bell. We thought we did something wrong, but we didn't know what it could have been.. It seems he was the tennis coach, and needed some young players. Tennis is the only sport in which I received instruction prior to beginning play. I was the only one of the three of us that had any interest, and continued with the team. My junior year I played singles and doubles. I was playing a fellow from Fleetside, and he was leading me 5–0. At that time you needed 6 games to win. I beat him 6–5. I few weeks later I learned that he had run away from home-but returned shortly thereafter. Over the years I saw a similar name in the newspaper when there were articles about golf. I often wondered if it was the same person, and he had given up tennis for golf. My doubles partner and I also were the county runners-up for the championship. This was quite amazing in that my school was never known for tennis since we certainly didn't have the excellent facilities as did many other county school districts.

I also was a drummer in the marching band. In my junior year I was elected president. This was a very valued position. The head of the music department didn't think much of my selection since I really wasn't a musician. I am the first to admit it. My thoughts also turned to girls at this time. I was very bashful and shy, however I became acquainted with a girl a year younger than me and it certainly helped to broaden my understanding of life!

At this time I got a part time job in the local supermarket. I also gave up my newspaper routes. This was very interesting, and exposed me to people older than me. I really liked the job, and the financial freedom it gave me. My brothers and I had always turned over most of my earnings to my mother, since we were not a wealthy family. In fact, as I look back, we were borderline poor. We never lacked for anything, but we sure didn't have very much. I mentioned the bicycle earlier. We, the boys, also got a baseball glove and that was about it. If we damaged or lost either, we had to buy the next one. For this reason, we always valued what we had.

By this time our family had grown from the three boys to six children. We had the addition of two girls, Alice and Marie, and a brother, Lee. Alice was 5 years younger than me, Marie was ten years younger and Lee was 15 years younger.

Note: These 5 year steps were very useful in later life when I tried to figure the age of my brothers and sisters.

We all had activities, we all went to Sunday school and church every week whether we wanted to, or not. Many sunday afternoons we would be playing football, and then we would hear 'Ricky, Fred, Gordon time for church'. Our mother always took us to church, I can't remember our father ever going to church.

I was now a senior, my brother Ken who was one year older than me has joined the Air Force. I was elected president of the student council. A very prestigious position, I really don't know why I was selected. I never made the Honor Society. I suppose my GPA was around 3.5. I now had a girl friend, my job at the market and I quit all sports.

I did continue to ski. I started skiing at age 14. At that time I took my Christmas money from my paper routes and bought a pair of skis. We had no local ski shop, just a sporting goods store. It had two pairs of skis. I bought one pair, and my cousin Tom bought the other. They were entirely too long for us, but what did we know? This reminds me of another story. I mentioned earlier that I played soccer. Here again, we all went to the local sporting goods store. I guess I got there after all the other players had gotten their shoes. I probably wore a size seven at that time. All he had was a size nine. I took them, and stuffed paper in the toe area. To this day, if I still had them, (and I do), they would still be too big.

During my senior year, when I turned seventeen and a half, I joined the Air National Guard. I really enjoyed the service, and thought of making it my career. I should mention that there was no money for college for any of us. My older brother Ken was very intelligent, as was Gordon, but we knew if we wanted college, we had to pay, or borrow. After joining the Guard, it didn't take me long to realize I had trouble taking orders from someone I didn't respect. The sergeant in charge, and several other sergeants were in constant conflict with me, I got along well with the officers and other members below the rank of sergeant I decided then that I better put in my eight years in the Guard and forget about making it a career. I graduated from high school in 1955. Several of my friends went to college, and some went into the service. I spent the next year working full time at the market. The spring of 1956 when Gordon graduated, our father came home from work one day and asked Gordon if he wanted a job in the steel plant laboratory. Gordon said he was going into the service, but I said I was interested. I got the job.

# 2

## *Into the Real World*

I was very lucky to get this job in the laboratory. An ex-teacher was my supervisor, so I had very good training. I was also exposed to various jobs throughout the plant, and was then asked if I would be interested in attending a technical school which had a co-op program. I went to school four weeks and then worked four weeks. This lasted for three years.. During this time I started going with other girls. In fact, a local hospital had a nursing school program. Every month a new group of girls would arrive. Several friends and I started frequenting a bar that was not too concerned about your age. I was about 19. We would go there almost every night to drink and dance.' A great time was had by all.' This was a favorite expression by my good friend Arthur.

If there was to be a raid by the state liquor enforcement agency, the bar owner was made aware, and we all left before the raid. I had that experience three to four times over the next two or three years. One Friday night two close friends of mine were at the bar. It was the birthday of one of them. Instead of going home after leaving the bar, they headed to another town. They hit a bridge abutment and one of them (Jim) was killed. He was a great guy, always kidding and smiling. He was also a sophomore at Penn State University. I also celebrated my 20 birthday at that bar. Perhaps it was fate that I celebrated my 20th birthday because the 21st would prove to be a sad day in my life.

With all this carousing, I didn't have much time to study, so my education suffered. I didn't fail, but I sure didn't do well. At this stage in life, two of my brothers were in the Air Force. My sister Alice was 15 and working at a local store. Marie was 10 and our younger brother Lee was 5. In the morning of Labor Day, 1958 my father was in the bathroom shaving. All of a sudden he called my mother. She came down the steps and called the doctor (at that time we didn't have 911). The ambulance came and took him to the hospital. He had a heart attack. I drove my mother to the hospital. We saw my dad. His only comment was he couldn't understand the doctor on duty. We left and went home. Early the next morning the telephone rang. My sister Alice answered. All of a sudden she started crying and said "daddy died". He was 45 years old. My mother took the phone, spoke for a short while and hung up. The next day I went with my mother to make the funeral arrangements. Ken had just finished his enlistment in the air force and was ready to start college in Texas. He came home, and the military sent Gordon home from Japan. Daddy died on a Tuesday, but he wasn't buried until Saturday because of the delay in Gordon getting back home. He was buried on my 21st birthday. The night before the funeral we had a viewing. I had been dating a girl, not too many times, but she showed up at the viewing. Later, she was to become my wife. She had never met my dad, but she told me she at least wanted to see him.

Our lives started going back into a routine for each of us. Ken went back to Texas to start college. He had to be convinced that going back was the best thing he could do, he thought he should stay home to help with the family. Gordon went back to Japan, I had my job and school. Alice and Marie had school and Lee was too young to know what happened. When I started the fall semester at the trade school, a week after the funeral, I was standing outside with one of my best friends when I just blurted out 'my dad died' and I started crying. I quickly stopped, but I left and went home. When I went back the next day everyone offered their condolences.

I finished the technical school, and was treated very well be my employer. My father had risen to foreman during his time at the plant. The owner lived out of town, but kept his car near our house. If I was outside when he came by, he would stop and ask about my mother, and how we were doing. He never spoke to me in the plant. Not only did he pay my tuition, he paid for the books and even gave me money for travel expenses to school. In fact, about a year into school, the workers at the plant went on strike for quite a few weeks. At one point, all the supervisors and managers were laid off, this included my dad. However, the owner kept paying my travel expenses to school. I felt very uneasy about that, but I was very grateful. After finishing school I was moved into other areas of responsibility in the plant. I really had it good for a 22 year old. I bought a motorcycle. I know my mother didn't like it, but like everything else in my life, she never told me what to do, or not do. (Note: as I look back, maybe she should have, although I probably would not have taken her advice). Back in the 50's, when you owned a motorcycle, your image really suffered. I didn't care, I really enjoyed it. I continued to own one for the next 40 years of my life.

At this point Alice was ready to graduate from high school and Gordon was coming out of the Air Force. He planned to go to college, as did Alice. She had been saving her money from working in a local store for several years. My mother had taken a job at a local diner. We got by, but I sure pitied my mother. In all the years my parents had been married, I never heard them argue. The worst I ever heard was one time when my dad was sick he told her he wanted hot soup. He sat down to eat it. He had a spoonful or two and said 'why can't you make this hot?" and went back to bed. He did like his alcohol. He worked second shift, and more than once I had to walk to the local fire company looking for him. Several times I had to help him back home. He never mentioned anything about these episodes, and neither did I.

In mid 1959 I came home for lunch, as I did every day, I was ready to go out the door, I turned and told my mom that I was going to get married, I don't even know if she had met Beth, my girlfriend.

We got married in January of 1960. We had a real fine wedding. We also had a wedding reception in the local Legion Hall. My one uncle told me on many occasions that we had the best reception he ever attended. The band cost us $35.00. We moved into an apartment and things were pretty good. I went out with 'the boys' on Friday nights. We always had a good time, but never got into trouble. On some Saturday mornings Beth would ask me why I was laughing in my sleep. I said I was remembering some of the funny things we did on Friday night. Beth worked on Saturdays. She was the secretary to the Merchandise Manager of a large department store located in Berkshire, the nearest major city, seventeen miles away. My close friends and I would play cards on Saturday afternoon (at the apartment). We also would go to the local meat market and buy the Saturday evening meal. When Beth came home we had steaks, potatoes, salad and dessert, all ready for eating when she walked in the door. A few months later we learned that Beth was pregnant She kept working and we prepared for the big day. Allen was born later that year. His birth forced me to start thinking about my future. Ken, Gordon and Alice were all in college. Where was I going? What was I going to do?

Although I didn't' do too well in the earlier technical school, I now had a desire to better myself. I enrolled in two night courses at a local college. I did OK and thought of continuing in night school. One of the instructors knew of my plans and suggested I go full time. Beth and I agreed. I left my job and in September of 1961. My supervisor at the plant asked me if I knew anyone who would be interested in taking my job. I checked with a friend of mine who said he would be interested. There wasn't much time between when I told them I was leaving and when I would begin college. It was solved through a version of the old adage,' tell me all you know in the next five minutes'. One of my duties was determining 'heat treatment' of the steel products. Without going into detail, you had the original condition, based upon this condition you then processed the product through various procedures to reach the desired condition. I wrote down all the required steps and alternate procedures for my replacement. Years later he told me that the guidelines worked fairly well. He had no prior exposure to the process before getting the job, but there were good, conscientious people employed in the department. Note: Five years later he married my sister Alice and became my brother-in-law.

# 3

## The College Years

I became a full time student with a major in chemistry. We moved in with Beth's parents. They lived in a semi detached, we had the third floor. I got a rural newspaper route to earn gas money. I worked from 4–6 A.M. six days a week. I traveled approximately forty miles each day. Because of the continual need for car repairs, I was lucky if I broke even paying for my transportation to college each day. Beth worked in a local state hospital. In April 1962 we had our second son-Randy. I was seven years older than the other people in my classes, and they really kidded me when they learned of our second child. The day after the birth I was back in class. Someone gave the instructor a note relative to my second son's birth, he acknowledged the fact and offered his congratulations. I was probably the same age as him. What may seem to be a somewhat trivial matter to most people, during the school year I received an invitation to join a fraternity. I sent back a note expressing my sincere gratitude for even being considered, but between my age, family and financial needs I asked to be dropped from consideration.

Around this time my mother began dating a gentleman from our home town. He was divorced, and none of us children knew him, but he was a hit from the start. He came to me and asked if we would mind if he saw our mother. None of us objected and I told him so. About 2 years later they married, and he became a close knit member of our family. I always hesitated to call him my step father because to me that carried a somewhat negative connotation and he was too good a person for that description.

During my college year I also started thinking about my next move. I really was interested in metallurgy since I wanted to continue working in the metals industry. The college I was attending was a liberal arts school, and didn't offer such studies, so I applied at Penn State University, 120 miles away. I was interviewed and accepted. At this time Gordon was also a student at that school. Beth and I decided I would go by myself the first semester, just to make sure I could do the work. I lived in the basement of a private home. I suppose I dressed 'more mature' than most students. I base this on the fact that during a snow storm I was walking to class and a car stopped and the driver asked if I wanted a ride. I was wearing an overcoat and carried my books in a briefcase. I got in the car and there were two other gentlemen. One introduced himself as a professor and the other two were also on the college staff. When I introduced myself as a student they were very gracious and offered me much advice. I did OK that first semester. I had no car, so I did a lot of walking all around the area looking for housing for Beth and the two boys. I finally found a spot in "Knob Hill Trailer Park". The next time I went home, always Greyhound, we went to a local mobile home dealer and bought a used unit. It was taken to the trailer park, and we now had a home! I worked as a shipping clerk for a publishing company, and a security guard for an electronics firm. This was the time of the Vietnam war. The firm was heavily involved in electronic surveillance. I normally worked the night shift and weekends. I also carried a loaded pistol. I had some training from my National Guard days, but I certainly wasn't very knowledgeable about using the weapon. Most weekends I had the job of checking the main headquarters and various other buildings located throughout the area. I was by myself. I often thought to myself, if I come across an intruder, what would I do? Lucky for me, it never occurred.

Beth got a job as waitress at the local Holiday Inn. This was a great help, financially. During football weekends she earned fantastic tips. She also had the privilege to serve many famous individuals and groups. Things weren't easy, but we did get surplus food from the federal government. It was the first time in my life that we actually had real butter. We got a lot of flour. I kept trying and trying to make bread, but I don't think I ever succeeded. About eighteen months after our arrival we found out that Beth was again pregnant. The first two deliveries required many hours in the hospital, prior to actual birth. Months later, one afternoon Beth told me she was more than ready for delivery. We put the two boys with a neighbor and we headed for the hospital. Beth was really near delivery as we were going to the hospital. I remember slowing down every time I saw an approaching bump in the road as we headed to the hospital. When we finally got there, I ran inside and they brought out a wheel chair. I believe she had Louise about two hours later. I now figured I better wrap up this education bit before we have more children Finally, after three years of going year round, I graduated. I had interviewed at three or four firms, but I accepted an offer from my prior employer back in my home town.

# 4

## *Into The Industrial World*

At this point, the Meyer family has four out of four with college degrees. Ken works for a national accounting firm, he recently received his CPA license. Gordon is working for the Federal Government, I can't mention where he works, or what he does! Alice is an elementary librarian and I've been hired as the Plant Metallurgist. Things were really going well. But I decided if there was never room for growth (for myself) I would move on. Beth and I sacrificed too much for me to sit in a job for 30 years and hope I would receive several promotions. The job was very interesting and I had a lot of independence to do my job. I became active in the industry's national organization. I traveled quite a bit and met many peers in my field. I had always been very bashful and shy. If someone talked to me, I could hold a conversation, but I never initiated a conversation with a stranger. I always felt I had nothing of interest to offer. It was only after earning the degree did I finally gain enough self-confidence to initiate conversations and to stand in front of several hundred people and make a presentation. After two years, I realized that I was going no where for the next 20 years. With the money I was earning and the independence I had, most people would have sat back and enjoyed the ride. I looked for another job. I found something about 40 miles away. After I accepted the job, I told my boss. He tried to talk me out of accepting the position. He told me how I could advance within the technical department. (Since I was the only metallurgist, this would mean a change of title every few years, and perhaps more money). It really would be the same job over the years ahead.

He told me there would be a lot of politics involved whenever opportunities arose. He also reminded me that I would have to be my own promoter. In a large organization you need a 'mentor' to watch out for you and help you gain proper recognition and advances. Note-I found this all to be hogwash!

Let me digress for a moment to make a point. Several months ago one of our grandsons was staying with my wife and me for a portion of his summer vacation.

He is only 14, but he is a very good conversationalist. He and I were talking about employment opportunities when you are in the active work force. Do you need a mentor? Do you need a personal defender? Must you play the political/self-serving card if you hope to succeed?

Normally, and I repeat 'normally', all of the above may help you. However, as I look back over my industrial career, I think that location and timing are much more influential. When an organization decides to expand or replace present employees—if you are already within the company—your possibilities of advancement are greatly improved. All this said, if you have shown that your capabilities exceed your present responsibilities, you are in a good position for promotion.

When I went with this new employer, I knew no one and no one knew me. One of the first assignments I received was to evaluate the steel melting procedures. I took the assignment for what is was. I didn't have to play favorites, I owed my loyalty to no one.

I observed all aspects of the activity. I talked to the foremen involved, and several of the workers involved. I then wrote my report and presented it to my supervisor and the Plant Manager. The Melting Superintendent and the Foundry Superintendent also received copies.

Within hours, there was a meeting in the Plant Manager's office. My supervisor thought the report was very good. The Melting Superintendent was very reasonable, but said that some of my comments were new ideas and he would have to evaluate them. The Foundry Superintendent was very upset. Who did I think I was to come into a large organization such as this and tell experienced people that their processes were outdated and inefficient I defended my comments and reasoning. I must state here that because of the freedom and independence given to me on my prior job, I was able to try new techniques, procedures and ideas. Many of them proved to be beneficial, and these are the recommendations I presented in this report.

Finally, the Plant Manager thanked me for the report. He liked the fact that my comments encouraged new thinking and a review of present practices. Conclusion of the report: Many of the ideas were incorporated into the standard practices. Also, the Foundry Superintendent and I became very good friends. Now, back to the main story.

This new employer was a very large company, relative to the average size of organizations in the industry. I would be Staff Metallurgist, with a significant increase in salary. Since the company was much larger, I figured there would be many more opportunities for advancement. The Department Manager was a very fine individual, but as typical for most metallurgists, he liked the paperwork and theory of the technical aspects of the position. My immediate supervisor was also a fine person. He had no degree, but a lot of experience. Things worked out well. He would tell me what he wanted and I did the job. It was very seldom that he would question anything I did. For myself, I preferred being in the plant, particularly in the melting area. For the novice, this was an area with large electric furnaces (50–75 tons capacity, the temperature within these units reach 3200 degrees Fahrenheit) and are used to melt steel.

Normally we melted 100,000 lb. every four hours. The steel was heated to 3000 degrees and poured into a 'ladle' (a large circular container, open at the top). From this container, the metal is poured into molds made of compacted sand held together with various types of binders to maintain a desired configuration. It is a very exciting, but dangerous area. Safety must always be the primary consideration. The company brought in a new Melting Superintendent when the present one retired. Here was a guy with experience, but he couldn't keep is mouth shut, or leave people do their job. Within six months he was out the door. The day he was fired, he and I were walking to the General Manager's office. He, to be fired, and me to be told I would succeed him. He told me what he made, and all the perks. This was to help me negotiate a salary and benefits. I told him that he should have just stayed in his office and let the people function, but he couldn't do that. He was always stirring up trouble and problems.

This was the job I really enjoyed. It was a three shift operation with a lot of responsibility. This lasted for about one year. At that time the company was bought by one of those individuals, so popular in the early 70's. The leveraged-buyout merchant. You have to give the gentleman credit. He bought a very profitable, private company employing approximately 1200 people. The company had a respected name in the cast steel and industrial equipment markets. He bought the company, and reportedly gave the family ownership a minimal amount of cash (which was already a portion of company assets), and the remaining obligations were to be covered from future cash flow. A new president also came in. A short time later my boss, the Plant Manager, tells me that the President is bringing in a friend to take over the melting department. I was transferred to the Marketing Department, and also served as Assistant to the General Manager. I had no trouble with the new Melting Superintendent, in fact he told me he had worked for the new President and both had lost their jobs. That is how he got to this position. Serving as the Assistant to the General Manager was very interesting. I handled annual budgeting and got to see quite a bit of financial information and sensitive operations issues. Many times I stood in the President's office while he screamed at the General Manager. I must say that he often deserved it. But he was an affable person. While working with the accounting people I also learned that the new owner was just draining all the cash from the company. There were no funds for maintenance or capital improvement. My Marketing supervisor took me to lunch one day, and said if he were my age (I was around 43) he would look for another job.

Instead of looking for another job, I started a small metals operation dealing with aluminum, brass and bronze. This was no conflict since my primary job was in the steel industry. I bought used equipment and got what is presently known as a home equity loan to finance the operation. A very good friend of mine, Will Miller, was a salesman for my prior employer, and he got me work from his customers who needed material made from aluminum, brass and bronze. It got to the point where I had more work than I could handle by myself. One day I took our oldest son Allen with me to my small operation. He was a big help, but the fumes were so bad, I then decided that I would drop this dream and stay in the corporate world. This was the first of many attempts to establish my own company.

A salesmen who called on my employer and sold products over which I had some influence relative to purchases, called me at home one evening. He knew of a company looking for someone like me, would I be interested? He named the company, and I immediately said yes. This company had an international reputation and wasn't too far from my home. It seems their prior Technical Manager had a drinking problem and had been dismissed. The temporary replacement had just had a heart attack, so they needed someone immediately. Because of the experience they had with the prior individual, alcoholism and radical behavior, when I went for the interview, it was me against approximately ten senior staff members. They all wanted to check me out, to be somewhat certain of what they would be getting. My present supervisor, the General Manager, knew many people with my potential, new employer, and I told him of my decision. He understood the necessity for my new employer to get someone quickly, so I left within the week. My last day on the job, the President asked me to stop in his office before leaving. He was very gracious, and said he was sure one of the reasons I was leaving was because he had brought in his own man. He told me that the new Superintendent told him that I had been performing very well, and he had not removed me for any weakness of my part. I thanked him for his comments and left for my new job.

By this time Beth was working as the Borough Secretary for a small community near our home. It was only four hours per day and she enjoyed such a position that required her to be dealing with people. Our children were growing. Both Allen and Randy were playing midget and mite (6–12 yr. old) football, and Louise was in elementary school. Things were just fine. I spent ten years with State Steel Foundry, I received several promotions and more responsibility. I was very active in national issues dealing with our industry, and also held several committee memberships on various technical committees. However, over the years it became very obvious to me that the company was not managed very well There was no accountability from anyone.

During the first few years with the company, I attended numerous meeting in which financial matters were being discussed. I had very little taining in accounting and finance, but some of what the attendees were told by the Treasurer didn't seem totally correct to me. A short time later I decided to earn some credits in financial subjects so that I could better understand some of these matters. I took these courses at a campus approximately 30 miles from my employment, and 60 miles from my home. I took four or five classes, and was thinking of ending this activity since I now had at least some basic understanding of finance. My faculty advisor was a visiting professor from Switzerland. He suggested I continue and earn my master's in Business Administration. This sounded very interesting to me. Since I was coming from an engineering background, I had to take about thirty ctedits just to enter the program. Overall, it went pretty well. I commuted two or three days a week, always during the evening. My thesis dealt with Quality Cost. The president of the company gave me full access to all financial and production information. The Treasurer had fought this accommodation to me, and I understand why. Let me mention just one point of financial controls that was of interest to me because of past experience. Allocation of costs provides the opportunity for excessive bias when putting together production cost information. When actual expeditures are demanded, there is little room for someone to influence the final numbers. It took me five years to earn my degree, but it was worth the effort. Over the years I was attending night school, I told many people that if I wasn't going to school, I would just be watching TV. I received my degree in the mail, while celebrating my fortieth birthday. As the senior Technical Manager (I was now VicePresident-Technical Services) I had constant complaints from customers relative to our product quality. At this time I started thinking again about owning my own company. I looked at a trucking firm, a motorcycle dealership and numerous other possibilities. But I really had no significant money for initial investment. Stories started to circulate that the company was going to hire a new president, from outside. This company was privately owned by two parties. A family member had always been the president. I called the President (his family owned 50% of the company) and asked for some time to speak with him. I went to his office and asked to be considered for the Presidency. Note: Remember my comments about my brothers and myself and the different thought we had each morning as we walked to the news stand to pick up our papers? They were concerned about safety, I looked for cigarette butts. Neither Ken or Gordon would ever have had the nerve to go to the president and ask to be his replacement. Never would they have offered themselves for the position. Is this pure arrogance on my part? I don't think so, it is just the personal traits of each individual.

The president didn't dismiss the idea, and said he would be back to me. The next day he said that the remaining owners, two of our customers, wanted someone from outside the organization. A new president was brought in, but he was weak, and in a weak position when it came to making tough decisions. He wanted maximum tonnage out the door, while the Vice President of Sales told me not to allow my quality people to ship anything which didn't meet all specifications. Neither I, or my people knew what to do when confronted with these opposing views. This situation continued for more than a year. Finally, one day prior to a Staff Meeting, the new president told me that I had to start shipping more product. I asked if he meant that we should relax quality levels. His comment, "you know what to do". The VicePresident of Sales looked at me and shook his head. I took the legal pad in front of me and wrote out my resignation. I walked to the head of the table and gave the note to the president. He had been discussing some subject, but paused to read my note. As I opened the door to leave the room, he called to me "hold on Rick, let's talk about this" I responded 'it's too late to talk" and went out the door.

That day was also the birthday of Randy. When we sat down for dinner I asked Beth how her day had been. She told me later that she knew immediately something was wrong because I never asked her such a question. I told the family, and said I'll start looking for a new job. At that point I had two mortgages (we had built a vacation home 3 years earlier), a wife and 3 children and-no job. Because of the national recognition of my now prior employer, I received job offers over the next two weeks. I decided to try consulting. I had a brochure printed and sent out several hundred letters offering my services. In a short time I had several opportunities for work. Some were foundries and some were casting users. It worked out real well. I charged $400/day plus expenses. Prior to that I was making about $50,000/yr. I worked two to three days a week and enjoyed myself. This continued for about six months.

Then one evening, got a call from the President of the American Division of an international company. I had met the gentleman on several occasions when he visited my prior employer. He heard I left and offered me a position with their American Division. I told him I was happy consulting and thought I would continue with this type of employment. He asked me to visit his plant so we could discuss possibilities. I made the visit. The plant was very fine, modern equipment with high productivity and a real commitment to quality. I again said I preferred the consulting business. His comment 'whenever you have free days, consult for me'. How good could it get! Whenever I had free days and wanted more income, I went to this plant. This was in another state, and transportation costs were significant. However, it was no problem since expenses were covered. Everytime I went to the plant the President would visit. His office was in Tennessee, and the plant was in southern part of the state, about 80 miles away. He always asked me to come work for him full time. Between all my consulting, I had a very good income and a lot of free days. It was difficult for me to change such a situation. However, after several months of such discussions I said I would take the job (VP Operations), but I wouldn't move until Louise graduated from secondary school. This would be about eighteen months. A deal was struck!

In 1982 we sold our home and moved to Tennessee. Allen was in the Marines, Randy at the University of Miami and Louise was starting at Arizona State University..

This was a very fine position. Excellent company, good equipment, very good people. I include both production and management personnel. You must remember, I came from the mid-Atlantic area to the deep south. I replaced a local person. However, I never really had any problems. In my dealings with people, I found they wanted their independence, but they were very committed to results. Very conscientious people. My staff was so good, I would come in around 7:30 AM, go into the plant and talk to the people on 3rd shift who were ready to leave and those on 1st, just coming in to work. I would read the WALL STREET JOURNAL, hold a meeting or two and then go back into the plant. I had many discussions with HR (at that time it was called Personnel) and Purchasing, but everyone did their jobs and I would normally approve their decisions. I went to corporate headquarters at least once a week to meet with the president. He was the best manager I ever served. He was a European, but very Americanized. There were several others from Europe, but most of them were much more conservative than the president. We added a new production department, and I also located another foundry which was purchased and made a division of the American group. The company also had a plant in Canada. At one point I was going there for at least one week each month. One of the president's closest compatriots managed this operation, but he was not a very good manager. I was the one who had to tell the president. The fellow was removed from the position and the company. He went on to form his own company in an unrelated business and did very well.

To be honest, I started to get bored. I didn't have enough to do, and no opportunity for advancement. However, the salary, bonus and perks were excellent. Since I was not of European background, there was no way I would take over the American Division even though my boss had higher goals.

In early 1985 the president called me to his office to help him celebrate the birth of his second son. When I arrived, we had a drink, and I then told him I planned to leave to buy my own foundry. My salary and options had allowed me to save approximately $400,000. This wasn't a lot, but it could get me started on an acquisition. He understood, but asked me to stay on until I found something. I hired an acquisition firm and started traveling all over the country looking at operations. In fact, I almost bought the foundry in my home town of Belmont from my old employer. In the interim he had sold it to a conglomerate, but they wanted to divest. He told a friend of mine (Will Miller) that I, Rick Meyer would be the new owner. Regrettably, the conglomerate sold it to one of their employees. I also was close to buying my old employer, State Steel Foundry. They were near bankruptcy and desperate for a buyer. My representatives negotiated, but they wanted the sky for a company ready to close the doors. They never knew I was the individual the acquisition firm was representing.

Near the end of the year, the president asked how I was doing. He asked me this everytime he saw me. I told him I would leave at the end of the year so I could spend full time looking.

I spent a full year traveling around the country, paying attorneys, accountants and many others as I searched for a purchase. Through out this time, Beth and I returned to our home area to visit my mother and her parents. One week end when we were in Pennsylvania., I reviewed the classified Business Opportunities in the local newspaper. I saw an advertisement listing a restaurant for sale. The next day I called the broker. He told me the details. It was a well known full service restaurant with rental units. It had a long and prestigious history. That night we went there for dinner. It was packed, and the food was good. Several weeks later we again went back to Pennsylvania and the restaurant. Same as the first time. I told Beth that we had to do something to protect our money. None was coming in and a lot was being spent for living expenses and my travel.

We made the purchase in May 1987. Randy and his wife and daughter moved to Pennsylvania with us. They both had restaurant experience from Tennessee. Randy had never made it through Miami. I pulled him out after two semesters. As I remember, all his courses showed an 'incomplete' for the final grade. Allen was out of the Marines and working as a maintenance mechanic in the area. Louise was out of Arizona State and teaching in Scottsdale.

# 5

## *The Pathway to Problems*

My nest egg was now almost depleted. A sizable down payment on the restaurant, eighteen months of living expenses, lawyers, accountants, etc, plus we bought a home. The restaurant business was very good. However, the profit we made was immediately put back into the business. It was very obvious the prior owners stopped spending on equipment and maintenance as soon as they put up the 'For Sale' sign, one year earlier.

Between the four of us, myself, Beth, Randy and his wife Kaye we were able to have some member of the family at the restaurant at all hours. Eventually, daily activities became routine and we all became familiar with the duties and obligations of ownership.

Then, one day, the opportunity to fulfill my life's dream became a very possible reality. It would also turn out to be the source of a life long burden.

One day I am at home and the telephone rings. It is the Chairman of a Florida firm that owned a foundry which I had looked at 2–3 years earlier. It wasn't much of an operation, but it had all the basic equipment. I was told that when I looked at it, they had an offer for a cash sale and that was why they never followed up with me. It seems the sale was never completed and they were again looking for a buyer. I told him I was interested, but I had put my money into a restaurant. This opportunity to own my own foundry would fulfill my life's dream. The question, how to accomplish this move. I told them I would see what I could do to raise some cash for a down payment. I talked to several banks and the representative of one of them told me to go to someone at a local bank that had just opened. They were very aggressive with their commercial loan practice. They agreed to lend me $150,000 against the equity in the restaurant. I contacted the foundry representative (Chairman) and told him of the possible cash available for the purchase, I then made arrangements to visit the company. I went to Florida, and then on to the plant. It looked very much like what I had seen when there two years earlier. My quick estimate was that I could reduce manufacturing cost by at least 10%. In addition, I expected to increase sales by 25–50%. I told them I was very interested, if we could work out a deal. Several days later he called back and said they were interested and would give me a $100,000 credit line to use until future sales generated some cash. This was a real gamble on my part, but this had been my dream since the day I left college. The present owner (a metal fabricating firm) had no idea as to how to manage a foundry. They had always had a manager for the operation, but could not keep anyone. They finally decided to sell and eliminate the problem and also the annual financial losses.

My personal philosophy has been, if you can live with the worst possible result, than make the move. If it did go into bankruptcy, I could accept that, therefore I told them I accepted the purchase terms.

Several weeks later I am on a plane to Washington DC (then on to Florida). A very good friend who had worked with me in the metals industry happened to be on the same flight. He asked where I was going, I told him, and I told him why. He was very happy for me since he knew it had always been my dream. He did indicate that even though he had his own dream, he could never take such a chance. He could not' live with the thought of potential failure'.

I was met at the airport and taken to the company's legal representatives. We had the closing, I handed over my check, and they immediately called the bank for verification. We then went to the plant and the Chairman left me there. I looked around, while standing in the middle of the plant. Now that I owned it, it didn't look as good as it did when I was just a potential buyer.

That evening I celebrated with a Big Mac, fries and several beers. The next day it was time to get to work. My plan was to stay in Florida for two weeks, and go home for the weekend. After all, I still had to keep an eye on the restaurant business. Beth was OK with people, but not with finances. Randy also had his own problems. I know that many times I drank more than I should have, but he seemed to be developing a routine of excessive drinking. Spending your work day in a restaurant with a bar was not the best scenario, especially since he stayed to close two or three nights a week. Kaye had the attributes needed to manage, she could discipline and also watch the dollars, but she could only do so much since they now had 3 young children.

The Florida operation started out fine, but very soon I realized that we had to reduce manpower until we increased sales. We had some very good months, and some very poor months. Sales were very erratic and there were continual equipment problems. This was an old facility relative to equipment. However it did have all the required equipment. I was using up my credit line very quickly to meet ongoing expenses.

My wife and mother came down one weekend for a visit. My mother was very proud, so was I. We were generating sales and customers were very good with timely payment. However, after one year, my credit line was gone, commercial banks would not provide such help, and the equipment had continual need for repair and or replacement. Business wasn't bad, but the unrelated expenses were killing me. Around this time we had extreme weather and the plant was flooded, this stopped production for more than a week. This happened again about six weeks later. I was starting to put my own money into the operation so that I could maintain production. I was continually using my credit cards to cover the payroll every Friday. There were many Fridays I wrote a check for at least $10,000 against my cash advance lines to cover the payroll prior to returning home for the weekend and a new set of problems at the restaurant The lack of funds to cover IRS payroll taxes became more or less routine.

One day, out of the blue, I got a call from a local machine shop looking for a foundry to produce castings for them. I met with the owner and we struck a deal for production. We received orders and started production. Now, a new problem arises. Production is increased to three shifts. We more than double manpower, plus, I now need a supervisor on each shift (2nd and 3rd). As you may well expect, manufacturing costs skyrocket, but shipments do not follow proportionally.

We have all new, untrained people. Even the people I put in charge have no real experience or training. I try to keep 2nd and 3rd shift obligations as simple as possible. Their only responsibility is to produce and process one product.

Employee problems develop. Many new employees quit. I estimate that at least half of the work force is on probation and they must leave the plant early every Friday to check in with their probation officer. Foundry work is hard, hot and dangerous. I go to the plant one night around midnight. Here is the 'supervisor' sitting in the office drinking beer. He's gone.

I scale back to two shifts. Several friends within the foundry industry call me, looking for a job. Most would have been a real asset to the company, but I couldn't afford them. Also, quite frankly, I didn't know how long I could exist with these conditions. Each week I am using my credit cards to get cash for payroll and general expenses.

We had the orders, but the 'learning curve' is always much longer than expected. In addition, running the equipment 12–20 hours per day is taking its toll. All the equipment is very expensive to repair. After 6–9 months I admit to myself that I can't continue with this situation.

I can't generate the cash flow to cover increased production, cover normal production costs and pay on the mortgage. I was cash poor, I was undercapitalized, which I knew beforehand. I went to the prior owner and told him of my situation. I couldn't continue, financially, with this situation. They didn't want to see me close the operation because the company would come back to them. For a similar reason they didn't want to see me in bankruptcy. They offered to take back 75% ownership. They liked the new business I was bringing into the company. I did not like this situation, but I didn't have much choice. (Exhibit No.1)

I did have the opportunity to get back 100% ownership, so I still had some hope. This new situation also limited my ability to pay company bills. Prior to this situation, when I had 100% ownership, there were several quarters when I was late with the withholding taxes due the IRS. Eventually I did pay all monies due, plus interest. Now this problem was to again resurface. There were several quarters I couldn't get approval to pay the taxes. I was told it was more important to pay suppliers so that we could continue to operate. Some of the taxes were later paid, with a minimal penalty. Some were not paid. Prior to this, when I still had total ownership, I had always paid, even though I was late. This condition was the start of my long path down the road of personal torment which would go on for more than 14 years. It got to the point were I no longer really ran the company. I was drawing a minimal salary while trying to manage the company out of its financial straits. The company had doubled the number of employees and tripled sales, but we were continually cash poor, with no help from the prior owner who now really controlled the company. I also had a visit from a local IRS agent investigating the missing tax payments. I told her of the contract between the majority owner and myself, relative to the need for their approval prior to issuing any checks. As President, she indicated that was my problem to resolve with the majority owner. Shortly thereafter I decided to leave the company and give up the remaining 25% ownership. My dream was dead, but my problems were just to begin.

September of 1991 I left the company. The enclosed letter covered my departure, (Exhibit No.2). Note that it states that my wife and I give up our ownership with the stipulation that Florida Fabricated. Products, the prior corporate owner, assumed all Florida Corp. liabilities. This was to negate any personal liabilities I had assumed for equipment purchases and any liabilities relative to the tax issues which I knew were an ongoing obligation. The flight back home was not very enjoyable, but I knew it was coming at least six months earlier. I thought my problems were behind me and I could now get on with my life. What a mistaken thought! Remember how I had rationalized my purchase by stating I could live with a bankruptcy, if it ever got to that point? I never reached that point, but as it would unfold, the situation I unknowingly would face would turn out to be much worse than bankruptcy.

I returned to Berkshire, leaving my life long dream in utter disarray. A day or two after returning, Will Miller called and told me that a new foundry had opened and they desperately needed someone with total foundry/management experience. This was a new operation started by a combination of entrepreneur, CPA and a gentleman (investor), none of which knew anything about a foundry operation. The entrepreneur knew Will, and the owner of my first employment. I called and got an interview with the CPA, he was the executive vice-president. I was offered the position of Manager. I asked for VP Operations. They really had no choice, so I got Vice President-Operations. The salary was $90,000. I was also asked if I was interested in investing in the company. This struck me as a very bad sign, relative to liquidity. It seems they thought I walked away with a bundle when I left Florida. If only they knew! By the time I left Florida I was into my credit cards for more than $150,000 for cash advances.

I worked for this company for 3 years, at which point they entered Chapter 11 bankruptcy. During this time I started to receive IRS letters. I believe the first was June 1992. This letter carried a liability of around $35,000. It got my attention. I was now making good progress on paying down my debt. Between the restaurant income and my new position I could put several thousand each month against the debt. After receiving the IRS letter, I decided I better get a tax attorney. My first mistake. I found this guy in the Yellow Pages. I made an appointment and went to see him. He was one of these 'You have a problem? Let's see what we can do'. I had mailed him a copy of the contract in which I agreed to giving up 75% ownership which had the stipulation limiting my ability to pay bills exceeding $5,000. I needed the approval of the Chairman and President of the company which took ownership of my stock. Depending of the cash situation when the funds (payroll taxes) were due, either we paid or not. Normally it was not pay due to the ongoing cash problem. I also sent him a copy of the September, 1991 letter (Exhibit No. 2) which stated that my wife and I gave up our 25% ownership with the stipulation that the acquiring company assume all outstanding liabilities.

The attorney. had forwarded this paperwork to the Philadelphia office of the IRS.(He moved the case from Florida to Philadelphia). While I was with him, he called the IRS office and spoke to a women. It sounded like they were old friends. (I wasn't to become part of that group). He put the call on speaker phone and she asked me my opinion of the matter. I told her about both pieces of paperwork, and felt the new owners and senior management were now obligated. She disagreed, and said I was the one obligated. I asked her how I should have handled the matter of prior approval before paying the bill, her comment was to the effect, 'Mr.. Meyer that was yours to resolve'.

July, 1992, I filed a protest to the basic tax obligation and the penalty. (Basically, they double the tax amount and call it a penalty).

I don't hear any more until June 10,1993. I had forwarded a copy of the Recapitalization of Florida Corp. (August, 1990), and a copy of the Plan of Reorganization of Florida Corp (The company had filed for Bankruptcy protection in mid-1992) dated October, 1992. Exhibit No. 1 and 3. I also submitted a copy of the Bankruptcy Disclosure statement dated October, 1992. (Exhibit No. 4)

June 1993, after an 11 month hiatus I finally get a reply to my protest. "You are obligated'. (Exhibit No. 5)

Correspondence, legal fees and frustration increases as the months go by. I write to the IRS, my attorney writes to the IRS, but nothing happens.

During this time I am talking to a contact I have in the finance department of the new (actually the prior) owners. I am told that the company has filed for bankruptcy. I tell my attorney. He calls the gentleman who has taken over as President. He acknowledges the filing and asked how we knew. That question wasn't answered by either of us. During this phone call the President told my attorney he would forward copies of the re-organization plan and the disclosure statements. I got a copy of both (Prior Exhibit No.3). After reading them I told my attorney that the company acknowledged in the filing that they owned 100% of the stock. Didn't this statement substantiate that they therefore assumed all liabilities as stipulated in my September 1991 letter? His comment was to the effect, 'well there's really no proof".

This exhibit also acknowledges the taxes due, a direct statement that the IRS could seize assets if the tax liabilities were not paid.

He writes a letter to the President of the company pointing out their statement of 100% ownership and my letter of September, 1991. He threatens them with legal action if there is no response. That's the last we hear from the Florida company.

In early June, 1993, I receive an IRS response to my protest of an earlier letter putting the full obligation for the funds due upon me. (Exhibit No. 5). In mid-February, 1994, my attorney calls and asks me to come to his office (Exhibit No. 6). October 4, 1994, my attorney sends a letter to the IRS stating I will not settle on a 50% basis. (Exhibit No. 7).

October 25, 1994, my attorney wants to talk to me about my argument relative to tax liability with the wording of my letter of resignation. Since I have no written proof of the company accepting my letter and terms, there is no confirmation. His second paragraph relates to the information I gave him that the corporation was making payments on the tax liability. Would they make such a move if they felt they had no obligation? (Exhibit No. 8).

About this time, I am without a job due to my employer's bankruptcy.

December 28 1994, (Exhibit No. 9). I get another threatening letter, telling me the new obligation is $40,000.

They tell me I can file a claim for a refund of $100 my attorney had me pay to them. (I really don't recall the purpose of this payment). If I want them to suspend collections while my suit for recovering this $100 is pending, I am told I must post a bond for 11/2 times the amount due. that would be $60,000. I didn't post the bond.

I also still owe about $100,000 on my credit cards and our restaurant business is starting to go downhill due to our location within the city. Crime is rampant, but really not in our area. Several regular customers tell us that they won't be coming back because they are afraid of being potential crime victims. Pointing out that we have not had any problems does not change their minds.

I start looking for a job. Over half the foundries in the area (thirty miles radius) have closed over the past few years. I'm almost 60 years old. I know people 50 years old who can't find work. Who wants someone who is 60? My two degrees really don't mean very much at that age.

I answered an ad in the local newspaper for a Quality. Manager. I sent my resume and received a call to come in for an interview. When I got there, a young lady was sitting in the lobby. While waiting, we had a brief conversation. It appeared that she had some background knowledge of the company and knew some employees. As a first for me, we are both called into the Plant Manager's office-TOGETHER. The manager describes the job duties and then tells me that the woman had worked for the company as a production worker and was presently on lay off status. The conversation went on for about 15 minutes. I was then asked to leave and wait in the lobby. When she came out, I was called in. The Manager told me that he had over 100 applications for the position. He had settled on me (years of experience and academic background) and the young lady who had experience in the production area. He asked if I was interested, to which I responded affirmatively. He asked the minimum salary I would accept. In my mind I had hoped for $40,000 minimum. I answered $30,000. He told me that it would be impossible to justify such a salary when others would work for much less. I left, and now realized the reality of my life and future. It didn't look good!

I receive a call from my contact in Florida.. I am told that the company is pay-ing on the tax obligation. She also questions why the company is paying if they have no liability. I inform her that the company is liable under terms of the re-organization where it is stated that they will pay all tax obligations over a 6 year period, or the IRS can file a claim against their assets. I inform my attorney and he contacts the Philadelphia IRS office to verify this information.

Exhibit No. 10. May 16, 1995. I get a letter from my attorney that he notified the Philadelphia office of the IRS that the corporation in Florida was making payments. Why didn't they all ready know that?

Exhibit No. 11. June, 1995. I get another letter threatening to levy. The amount is now $42,000. It tells me to pay in 30 days!

Exhibit No. 12. June 25, 1995. I write a letter to the IRS. A month later I get a letter from them stating that they asked the Florida Office to respond to my let-ter. (Exhibit No. 13), dated July 17, 1995.

August 14, 1995. (Exhibit No. 14). I get a letter acknowledging the payments by Florida, and stating that as long as payments are received, they will stop harassing me.

I drop my attorney.

At the end of 1995, Florida stops making payments to the IRS. They made about six payments. The bankruptcy papers stipulated that if Florida Corp. didn't fully cover all tax liabilities, 'this class of priority claimants shall be entitled to enforce their pre-petition claims as if no Chapter 11 proceedings had been filed and confirmed'. In other words, when they stopped payments, the IRS could have demanded full payment. If not met, they could have seized any/all assets. Just as they were doing to me.

In addition to these problems, it is becoming very evident that we must do something with the restaurant. We had hoped to eventually sell it to our son and his wife. However this would not work for two reasons. We were losing business, no matter what we tried. People from the suburbs were going to all the newly opened nationally franchised units rather then risk driving into the city. These people represented more than half of our week end sales. Weekday sales came pri-marily from the local neighborhood and these sales were holding up. However, our son had developed a problem with alcohol and I heard stories of drug usage. We decided to put the restaurant up for sale.

By July of 1996 I had tried several methods to generate more income. I started working with a fellow who had started a Manufacturing Representative business. He was representing quite a few manufacturers, but had not generated any sales for them. Manufacturers Representatives only make money (5%) when they generate sales for the manufacturers. I visited many potential customers, but as expected, the majority were going off-shore to make their purchases.

I also opened a take out business for the evening meal. We prepared all the food in the restaurant kitchen. I then took it to the retail outlet using insulated containers to maintain the hot temperatures. We were hoping to catch the commuting mother, and father, who would stop to purchase a wholesome meal at reasonable cost, rather than go home and spend time preparing such a meal or settling for junk food or pizza. We had very loyal customers, just not enough of them to cover our cost. My original business plan called for the restaurant kitchen to serve five such outlets. I didn't have the cash to open more than one unit. Approximately four months later I closed "My Kitchen". Note: Prior to start-up I talked to an representative for an investment group. They liked the idea, but wanted to see me prove the concept before investing. One has to wonder how much investing these people made with such limitations as to where to put their money.

I kept plodding along, trying to take care of all the financial obligations for the restaurant and my personal obligations. I started falling behind in restaurant water bills, local taxes. state sales taxes. Somewhere I found the money to cover them before they became too great. Isn't it ironic in that when you have no funds to pay a bill, you must now pay even more to settle the obligation? However, I can offer no alternative.

We are now into 1997. This will prove to be the worst year of my life. It almost was the last year of my life.

January 6,1997. Final Notice to levy. The total is now $48,255.00.(Exhibit No. 15). Another 'Final Notice'. How do you respond to something like this? What do they want me to do, print the money? I understand their viewpoint. They want the money, they don't really care who pays.

Emotion, compassion and reality don't enter into IRS decisions. Wait-I say decisions? They really don't make decisions. Everything is preprogrammed. Do you really think that prior to sending such notices that someone will review the form, make certain it is accurate and check to see if there is any activity with the account? Speaking as one who has been on the receiving end of many such notices, the answer is NO!

This is the result of what is known, and well recognized as 'the beauracracy'. This is somewhat like a train going down the track. Even if someone somewhere looked into this matter and concluded that maybe Mr. Meyer does have an argument, what can they do? The majority of these forms are automatically generated.

How do you stop the entire system? It can't be done-even if you wanted to investigate all the presented issues.

(Exhibit No. 16) January 18, 1997. I send another letter to Philadelphia IRS. This letter points out to the IRS that they keep billing me for the total amount, even though Florida Corp. has been making payments on the account as specified in the bankruptcy proceedings. I also point out that I have learned that Florida Corp. no longer exists. The ownership closed the company and has emerged with a new name. Apparently the IRS has no knowledge of this. How can this be? Why didn't they invoke their right to seize assets when payments were prematurely stopped? They knew nothing about this change, and therefore took no action. You see they (IRS) had no reason to act, they always had Rick Meyer.

February 7, 1997. (Exhibit No. 17). I receive a letter stating that the Philadelphia Problem Resolution Department is looking at my problem. It seems the Problem Resolution Program corrects problems that have not been resolved through regular IRS contacts. These people must be awful busy considering the lack of input by normal channels.

April, 1997. (Exhibit No. 18). Final Notice to levy. We now owe $50,000. Gee, another 'Final Notice'. These notices get to be a goulish joke. What do they think you will do? Do they think that by some magical event I will now have $50,000 laying around that I can use to pay them? I didn't have $48,000 to pay the bill three months ago. They must have heard the local rumor that I won the state lottery and they better get their share before it is all spent in Las Vegas. This is a joke! No such luck.

May 19, 1997. (Exhibit No. 19). I send a letter to Senator William Roth (DE.). Back in the mid-nineties, Senator Roth was conducting an investigation into the collection methods used by the IRS. I decided to send my story to him. My correspondence was what could be considered an outline for this book. In fact, it was while I was gathering information for the letter to Senator Roth that I started giving thought to writing this book.

I had no response from Senator Roth, none was expected.

June 1997. (Exhibit No.20). The Resolution Department says I am the only company officer liable for payments. No reference as to whether they looked at all the earlier correspondence and bankruptcy information that has been referenced.

Note: In 2004 I met with another tax lawyer. I wanted some advice as to how I could proceed on this matter. I wasn't going to pay him a retainer to be my advocate. First of all, I couldn't afford it at that time.(This situation will be covered when the story gets to 2004). He read the documents concerning the background information and said that Florida Corp. accepted my stock and therefore accepted my stipulation relative to the tax obligation. That was his opinion, at this point there was really nothing I could do.

The following summary highlights my contention that the liability should have been paid by Florida, Corp. Available information to justify my contention:

1. Agreement covering prior owner when they assumed 75% ownership. Rick Meyer limitation relative to writing checks.

2. Letter covering the resignation of Rick Meyer and his returning of 25% ownership to Florida Corp. with liability stipulation.

3. Florida Corp. re-organization plan identifying Florida Corp. as 100% owner of stock.

4. Bankruptcy disclosure statement stating that Florida Corp. will make 72 monthly payments to cover federal tax liabilities. If not fully paid, IRS or any other creditor can file against assets of company. The company made seven payments.

June 12, 1997. (Exhibit No. 21). I receive a Transaction Sheet. This shows a time table of monies due and monies paid. This paper shows that Florida Corp. made seven payments of $2200.00, approximately $17,000. The time period was January, 1995 to October, 1995. If you remember, they were to make 72 payments. The IRS took no action to collect any more funds. They came back to me.

I am now in a state of total depression, we have to do something with the restaurant. There have been many 'lookers', but no one with sufficient down payment to make a transaction fairly secure. I now also have a new problem to consider. My mother has been living alone in my hometown ever since her second husband was killed in an industrial accident. She had worked in the local school cafeteria until 65 and then retired. Note: She later told me that this was the biggest mistake of her life. She had been very active in the community until the early nineties when she had multiple bypass surgery. At that point her doctor told her to slow down and drop her community responsibilities. She did this, and even though her health was good, she now had nothing to do. Note: She also told me that she should not have listened to her doctor. However, now that she had dropped everything, she said she would feel very uneasy if she tried to go back into her prior organizations.

Now, in 1997, about 3–4 years after her operation, she calls me and says someone is in her house. I make the 45 min. drive to her home and show her that no one is there. She tells me there are two people sitting on her sofa. I see no one. Later, my two sisters tell me this isn't the first time she has seen these 'visions'. This is just the beginning. She continues to 'loose' her purse and keys. She is still driving, and we question the wisdom of that. My two sisters live nearby and they are at her home on a daily basis to take care of her needs.

My mother starts calling the police and tells them people are in her house. We all ask her to come live with us, each of us have plenty of room. She resists, she doesn't want to bother any of us looking out for her. She will stay in her own home. Events start to get real bad for mother. My one sister gets the name of a private psychiatric hospital which is 50 miles from her home. We get an appointment with a psychiatrist and I take mom to meet with the doctor. The first thing he does is dramatically reduce her medication. She was taking about 8 different pills multiple times each day. He cut that amount by more than one half. We started to visit this doctor every month. She really didn't seem to improve.

I remember on one visit the doctor gave her a memory test. He told her a very brief story of two people starting their day, traveling to one or more to spots, eating their meals and returning home. He then asked her questions pertaining to the story. Keeping my own score, I got around 60–70% correct. Mom correctly answered about 10%. I was afraid to ask him what per cent correct answers was considered passable. After several months he told me that she had signs of dementia (to me this means Alzheimer's disease), and told me that it was not Alzheimer's-at this point We now knew that we had to get her into a home, if only for her own personal safety, we couldn't let her live by herself. My sisters and I had attended a one day seminar for people caring for someone with Alzheimer's. I couldn't believe some of the stories told by people. This next comment isn't meant to be funny, and it's the guideline that guides me into the future. There is nothing wrong with forgetting, or losing your keys. When you find them and don't know what to do with them, it's too late. This statement was offered at the conference.

We visited several homes with her and surprisingly at almost every home we visited, she knew somebody staying there. She finally agreed to enter a home near her home town. There were many people there who she knew. We thought this would be good for her. Note: It turns out that even when she was admitted, while in very good physical health, she never really was aware of the people around her. One day shortly after she was admitted, we were visiting with her in the community room. There were many other people, visitors and residents, in the room. Mom looked at one women and complained about how she seemed intolerant of other people. It was very unusual for our mother to speak like that about anyone. She said she didn't know the lady, but didn't like her. It turns out it was her room mate. But as far as she was concerned, and told us, she had her own room.

Along with these problem, my wife and I were having a very difficult time. Calls from creditors bothered both of us. Beth was very defensive about our son and his problems. In addition, Beth was having continual problems with arthritis. She had so much pain, but she very seldom mentioned it, I could see her pain. We both saw the signs of problems. Randy's wife Kaye spoke to us about his problem-what could she do?

I have never spoken to any one about the following subject, but it has to be mentioned since it played a major role in my efforts to solve all my problems. I started to think about suicide. I had sufficient insurance coverage to pay all our debts, including the tax problem. I now also had a tax liability from the restaurant. I admit to this obligation, and it was much less than the Florida problem. We owed about $5K for the restaurant. I missed a quarterly payment. If I accomplished this mission (suicide), Beth could pay off everything, have a small nest egg and own property with a value of at least $750,000. No more worries for her. This wasn't an emotional decision, it was a business decision. As stated by Andy (Tim Robbins) in the Shawshank Redemption, 'Get on with living, or get on with dying'. I was 60 years old. The restaurant couldn't' carry itself anymore, I couldn't find a meaningful job. Beth and I are constantly fighting, about everything. Randy has got to get out of this atmosphere so he can straighten himself out, and I just can't go on like this. I knew many people who were better than me and had died at an earlier age. Perhaps this was to be my time.

I had a very good friend who had attended the same technical school I went to back in the fifties. Over a two year period he tried to get me to attend metals industry outings with him. It would have been very enjoyable, but I always found an excuse not to go with him. I don't know if he knew anything about my problems, or if he just wanted my companionship. I suspect that he really didn't know of my problems. I never got to speak to him after late 1997, I guess he gave up on me.

I started thinking about how I could kill myself and make it appear as an accident. A car accident, drowning. If I did anything, I wanted it to be final. I sure didn't want to end up a vegetable. Relative to the drowning, I did a lot of running by a river. I thought I look for a spot where someone might accidentally trip and fall into the water. I had all sorts of thoughts. How about hanging, suffocation, CO poisoning with the car? As I would drive to and from the restaurant I started looking for places were I could ram my car into a tree or pole. If you notice, on most highways there are barriers at bridge abutments. I found several good sized trees along the road near my home, but I kept thinking about an imperfect hit and not killing myself. One afternoon I decided to go running along the river, and just throw myself into the water. I waited until evening when it was just turning dark, I thought at this time no one would be around the park. I had picked out my spot earlier. As I approached I noticed several people in the area, walking both ways. There was no way I could do it under those conditions. I ran up the trail and came back. Again, people are in the area. I gave up and went home. Next try coming up.

All of this was taking place in early December 1997. I even tried to make my plans so that Louise wouldn't be too inconvenienced. She and her family would have to come in from Nevada. If I did it early in the week, they could be back home early the following week. I next tried suffocation. This is really horrible. It was early evening, I was home alone with the dog. I took a plastic bag and went into the back yard. We had no neighbors within 300ft and the property was surrounded by trees. I sat down and put the bag over my head, and taped it shut with masking tape. Within 5 seconds there was no more oxygen, I couldn't stand it—I ripped the bag from my face. Several nights later I thought of carbon monoxide poisoning with my car. I couldn't do it, at least not in the garage. Beth would probably never go into the garage anymore and who would buy a house were the owner killed himself? I now thought of hanging. I found a tree in the back of our property. It was really on the neighboring property so that satisfied my concern of being on my property. I picked out a limb, I swung on it, I hung on it with all my weight and did everything possible to check it out. This was a Friday night. It was around 5PM, it was nearly dark. First I typed goodbye letters to Beth, my children, my siblings and my grandchildren. My major concern was the grand children. I didn't want them to think that suicide was the way to solve your problems, but in my situation it appeared to be the only choice. I was serious and humorous in all the letters. I told them I knew exactly what I was doing. I apologized if this would embarrass them in any way, and I apologized to Beth for getting us in this situation. I really didn't know if she could handle this, but she would have the grandchildren to love and cherish. I got the rope I had prepared, and my dog and I went to the tree. The dog just sat and watched me. I put the rope over the limb. There was a rock nearby, approximately 2 ft high. I put it under the limb and stood on the rock and tied the rope to the tree. I then tied the rope around my neck, it was taut with the limb. I stood there on the rock for a minute or two and thought about what I was about to do. Is it right, or wrong? I had already made that decision. I jumped off the rock. The next thing I knew I was laying on the ground with a broken limb on top of me. I estimated I was out for about 10–15 min. based on my watch. I felt OK, but I had a burn on my neck from the rope. I have no idea how/why that limb broke. I had checked it in every way.

I told myself, it was meant to be. Now you better get to the restaurant before they start wondering were you are. I went in the house and looked at my neck. It had a red mark from the rope. I put on a collared shirt and sweater to somewhat hide the mark. I went to the restaurant, the kitchen staff kidded me for being late, I was the dishwasher for the night.

I continue to struggle, tying to figure out what I can do. There appears to be no way to handle all the financial obligations. March 23, 1998. I receive an IRS notice that we owe $6,000 for the restaurant for the 4Q1997.

April 20, 1998. I type several notices and hang them on the restaurant doors. 'Restaurant closed, thank you for your patronage'. Now I have to get all the tenants out of the rooms and apartments. This takes about four weeks. In the meantime the prior owner and mortgage holder files for repossession. I expected this. I had no problem with him, but my action resulted in a loss of about $300,000 in equity in the property. On the other hand, since I never could find a buyer, how much did I really loose? I do know I lost my opportunity for a nice retirement. We now had nothing.

I located an attorney who seemed to be very knowledgeable with situations such as ours. We filed for personal bankruptcy. This is a very demeaning experience, even if you are the only one who knows what you are doing. We found a buyer for our home, that pays off the two mortgages and resolves that matter. Beth finds a rental property that is really nice. I also now make a real effort to find any kind of a job. I end up with a temporary service. They get me a job in a machine shop. I am a machine operator. It's an OK job, but it only pays $7.50 per hour. Several weeks later I notice an advertisement for a laboratory technician. I send them a very watered down resume. I decided I had more of a chance if I greatly minimized my past experience. Who would hire an ex-VP of Operations for a technician job? Without thinking about it, I had listed my BS degree and graduation date. This date was 7 years after someone directly out of secondary school would have graduated from a four year program. Thereby implying I was seven years younger than my real age. I was called in for an interview. When I received the call, the HR representative asked me if I really was interested in such a position. I answered affirmatively. Note: I had been out of the employment market so long, I thought HR was the initials of someone in Personnel—the old name for HR.

When I got to the plant, they gave me an application to complete. It only went back something like 10–15 years, therefore it gave no indication I had worked for 7 years before going to college, again implying I was seven years younger. I got the job. What always amazed me was the fact that no one in the company (they employed about 800 people) knew me, or at least didn't come in contact with me. It wasn't a bad job, and it did offer a lot of overtime. My income was around $50,000/year.

Beth worked part time, but she was having severe problems with her arthritis. She had a lot of pain in her hands and her hip area.

August, 1998. The local IRS office sends me a notice to come in for a meeting relative to the restaurant tax problems. They wanted to know how we got into such a situation. I told them the Florida story and the restaurant story. Business was declining, I couldn't find a second job and I decided to pay the suppliers rather than the IRS. If the suppliers were not paid there was no restaurant business. That would put 15–20 people on unemployment.

We don't hear anything from anyone until January, 1999. We get a letter to come to the local IRS office again. We go in and complete a 'Collection Information Statement'. After it is completed, the agent tells us that our income is not great enough for them to garnish any of my wages. At that point I ask him about the Florida. situation. I am told that Florida had written it off as 'Uncollectible', however Philadelphia had it as an active file. Lucky for me when my attorney switched the account from Florida to Philadelphia! We never did get any official response to the Collection Form we had completed. That's the way they always work. They never tell you anything, except what they want to tell you. Our lives continue, but with the problems always in our mind. I admit to the restaurant obligation, but not Florida

It is now late in the year 2000. We have come through the millennium, but mom is really in poor condition. As she started going downhill, more than once she indicated to me that if she had a choice she would end her life. She had no life. A women who raised six children, was always active, now lays in a bed with essentially no knowledge of her surroundings. I realize there are many people who oppose euthanasia, I am not one of them. How can anyone with a sense of decency and respect allow someone they love to have to endure such an existence? In the end she was just a small body curled up in the bed. She couldn't speak, she didn't open her eyes, she was in her own cruel world. I went to see her one day after work. I just stood and stared at her pathetic existence. I put my hand on her forehead and then walked out of the room Our oldest son Allen visited her the next morning. We are told that she died a few minutes after he left. In fact, the staff thought he was a minister. They said they saw him kneeling at the end of the bed and praying for her. Life goes on.

In mid-2001 I started to look into the possibility of buying another home. The bankruptcy had been discharged in 1999. I found several mortgage banks on the Internet. I was surprised to learn how receptive they were. I had bought a new vehicle in late 1999, just after the bankruptcy discharge with minimum down payment and a 9% interest rate. That didn't seem too bad to me. We found a nice small home that was 3 years old. We got a mortgage at 9.25%. Somewhat high, but if we made consistent payments for 2 years, it would automatically drop to 8.25%. Well, at least now I had a job, and a home. I also was able to again start saving for my retirement years.

I was now 64 yr. old. Most people are ready to wrap it up at that age, or before, I wasn't to be so lucky, but my health was good, and I really didn't think I was ready to retire.

August 26, 2002. (Exhibit No. 22). We get another 'Final Notice' with Intent to Levy. We now owe $62,000. Who really knows what we owe? I have no idea, and I am certain the IRS isn't going to take the time and effort to document everything for me. 'Send your full payment today'. Yes, it's on its way! They enclosed an Appeal Form. I have just turned 65 and have begun to receive social security payments. I am banking this money for future retirement needs.

September 3, 2002. (Exhibit No. 23). I send a letter to the IRS and offer to accept some type of payment plan. I also filed the Appeal Form.

In late 2002 I get a telephone call from a very large company in the metals industry. They ask if I would be interested in a consulting opportunity covering several years. They plan to add a new division and I was recommended. The fee would be $1200/day, plus expenses. They would expect me on site for at least 10 days each month. Talk about good luck! Who would believe this? I compared 2 years of this work with my present situation, and there was no comparison. I accepted the offer and resigned from my present job. I told them I was retiring.

March 2, 2003—I was working 12–14 days per month, and the preparation for building the new plant were well underway. Things couldn't be better. I came home on Thursday one week, when I got a call from the Vice President who hired me. Bad news. The Board of Directors canceled the project and would buy the product off shore. Here we go again.

Instead, I decided to really retire. I got into the yard work. I enjoy such activities. Two weeks later, the outside work is all completed. I was also running every morning, instead of two times each week as I did while working full time. After about six weeks of running every day, it didn't provide near the amount of enjoyment I had when running two times each week.

I am not any good at golf. There is no way I could play golf three to four times each week. What am I to do? I expect I would have become the best conditioned alcoholic in the area if I continued with this routine. I had started to drink a few beers in the late morning, followed by a few in the late afternoon. I didn't want to get on that ride!

I started looking into part time work. I could drive a school bus! Not me. Early in my life I knew I could never be a school teacher. (After several weeks of teaching, either I would be gone or there would be no students left in my classes. I am too much of a disciplinarian).

I got an offer to work as an Adjunct Professor at a Community College. I would teach two courses. However, it was about sixty miles from my home.

At this time I also answered an advertisement from a temporary service agency looking for production workers in the metals industry. I interviewed with the temporary service and she set up an appointment for me. Remember, I am now 65 years old. I interview with HR. The gentleman noted my background and said they might be able to use me in the Research area. I interviewed with the Research Director and get the position of laboratory technician. It's an entry level type position, but it's a job.

In early 2003 we receive an Offer In Compromise form. I had never heard of such a thing. It stated something to the effect that since we had paid our personal taxes, on time and fully, for the past three years we were eligible to submit this form. In essence, we offer to pay a portion of the total amount to settle the case. I competed the form and provided all the necessary paperwork and documents. I then mailed the forms. (Exhibit No. 24 and 25). Note: I believe this form went to somewhere in New York. I have now dealt with Florida, Philadelphia and the local office, and New York. I am certain the unsigned notifications came from other locations. It is also apparent that one office never communicates with the other.

July, 2003, I get a letter from the Appeals Office relative to my filing of Sept 2,2002. (Exhibit No. 26). It states that they will be asking for more information to support the information in my file. It also says 'What you can do'. Answer: Respond quickly if asked for addition information.

August 5, 2003, I request a hearing. The IRS sends me forms 433 A & B for completion. I submit Form A since they are addressing the mail to me alone. (Exhibit No. 27). This always means that they are talking about Florida.

I am now starting to work on saving funds for my real retirement. I have a 401K, a savings account and money in the stock market. I pay off my truck which permits me to save even more money.

May 21, 2004. The IRS rejects my appeal and Offer In Compromise. They state "there is no doubt as to my liability. Relative to the OIC, 'Rejected since I had many more assets than I offered as payment'. I had listed $30,000 in a Certificate of Deposit, but did not offer this toward my payment offer. I had stated in the paper work that this money was being held to pay capital gains tax on a property we had recently sold. This already was government money. My tax return for 2002, filed in April of 2003 reflected payment of this money. I now know a lot more about OIC and realize I should have offered more money toward the settlement. All I knew was what I saw on TV. 'We settle for $.10 on the $1.00!'

There was an interesting statement with this letter. (Exhibit No. 28 and 29). 'You are not eligible for an Installment Agreement because of your inability to pay within the Statute of Limitations.'

Around June 2004 I get a call from a gentleman in the Resolution Appeals Office. He tells me that the statute of limitations expires at the end of 2004. Therefore they can not allow me to make installment payments. (This Florida case has been ongoing since 1991, 13 years!). He asks me the value of my liquid assets. I tell him $25,000. He tells me that is what the IRS will want to settle the claim. He also tells me to complete Form 433 A and then go to the local IRS office. I obtain the form, complete it and go into the office. As a matter of information, you can't call a local office. You can dial the number, I found it on the Internet, but you must leave a message.

I tell the woman standing at the counter why I am there. I show her the form I completed and tell her about the telephone conversation I had with the Appeals Resolution Office. She indicates she has no knowledge of what I am talking about. She takes the form and goes to talk to someone. She scurries back and forth between me and someone in the back (behind the curtain). Something like the Wizard of Oz. She finally comes to the counter and tells me to leave the paperwork. They will get back to me.

On July 19, 2004 I receive (Exhibit No. 30). She has sent me a hand written note telling me to liquidate my stocks, IRA and 401K and forward the money to the local office. I was also told to complete another 433 form.

I cash in my IRA, my stock fund and close a savings account. I then debate with myself how to handle this check for $26,000.

A few days later I receive a call from the women at the local office. I am now told to pay the $26,000, plus $1650/mo for 40 months. I sent a letter dated August 5,2004. (Exhibit No. 31). I have no idea how she arrived at her number, and it is in conflict with the numbers from the Appeals Office. She also wants me to complete a Financial Statement for 1997/1998. I no longer have information on that time period, and no idea how I can complete the form.

She then sends me a note dated September 14, 2004 (Exhibit No. 32). This note tells me that the statute of limitations is now February 29,2008. Who really knows what is happening?

On September 22, 2004 I receive a new note. I must decide if I want to file a new OIC or request a payment plan. (Exhibit No 33). Attempt to remember this date. A year later I will learn that I can't file another OIC, and recall that the Appeals office said I couldn't request a payment plan because of their information relative to the statute of limitations.

I decide to call a tax lawyer with the legal firm that handled our bankruptcy. I basically despise all lawyers, but our abankruptcy lawyer seemed to have a true concern for our personal feelings during this period. I wanted some advice as to what I should do. I met the tax attorney. He certainly didn't show the empathy of the bankruptcy attorney. First of all he seemed to be more interested in getting the hourly fee than he was in discussing my situation. He spends the majority of the hour telling me how he grew up in an affluent family and just couldn't understand how I could have taken such gambles. I left his office and mailed the check to him as soon as I got back home.

I decide to present the check as payment toward the restaurant obligation. At this point I have been told that statute of limitations for Florida Corp. will end December 31, 2004. Note: I believe the Appeals Office more than I believe the woman at the local office. It is now October, 2004. Why should I pay on the Florida Corp. obligation? I submit the check for payment to the restaurant account. (Exhibit No. 34).

I point out that I don't know which office to believe. The Appeals Office tells me I owe a total of $54,000. This represents Florida and the restaurant. They also say the statute of limitations expires at the end of 2004. The local office wants approximately $90,000 over 40 months. They also say the statute of limitations expires April, 2008. I figure I will pay off the restaurant, amount and continue the fight about Florida.

I didn't hear anything relative to the check. I check my account, and it has not been cashed. This continues for about three weeks.

Finally, on October 16,2004 (Saturday), we receive the mail. There are two certified letters from the IRS. One tells me they have put a lien on our home. The other says they are garnishing my wages. (Exhibit No. 35). On Monday the 18th we get a call from the bank. The IRS has frozen my checking account .Recall that

I had closed all my accounts. I put the money into my checking and sent them a check for $26,000. This check was never cashed.

Also on Monday, my employers' HR department called me and told me about the garnishment. It turns out they take a little more than half of what I was netting prior to the garnishment I also called my banker and he told me that they were to hold the funds for 21 days and then forward them to the IRS. The total in the account is nearer to $30,000 since it also contained funds for normal monthly bills.

I then call a telephone number listed on the notices I had received. The office is in Pittsburgh, PA. Another new contact! No human answers the phone. I am told I may contact their office through a Fax number. I send them a letter giving my viewpoint of the entire matter. (Exhibit No. 36). I never have received a response.

My account is now empty. I have electronic payment for essentially all my monthly bills. My November 1 mortgage is due. I put sufficient funds into the account to cover the bills coming due. In the afternoon of November 1, I call to check on my account balance. It is somewhere around $23,000 short. It seems the IRS presented my $26,000 check for payment on Nov. 1. This caused any and all other due payments to be refused due to insufficient funds. I had funds in the account to cover my normal bills and the IRS check. They freeze the account and then present the check for payment. Are they really such terrible people, or is it the ongoing case of one office not knowing what the other is doing? I have my opinion.

I call several IRS numbers available to me to see what I can do relative to the lien and the garnishment. I also file another Appeal. This Appeal includes a lot more information (evidence) as to why I don't feel I owe this sum of money. I don't expect much from the presentation. I call the collections department (I really don't know where they are located. One paper indicates Kansas City). They know nothing of the check I submitted, or the garnishment. I am told to make an offer of a payment amount. I offer them $800/mo. I am told that their figures indicate I can pay $1600/mo. At this time I didn't know what the garnishment was going to be. I tell them my age and the need to prepare for the time when I can no longer work. This has no credence with them. Over the years I have read about how people have settled for 25–50% of amount due. How do they do that? I suppose if you can afford it, you get a good law firm for representation.

Around mid November I come home from work and my wife says I am to call the IRS. Now what? I call the number, then you wait, while waiting you get this speech about don't hang up or you wait even longer when you call later. Finally I get a young women on the line. I told her I was to ask for Jack White. She tells me that there are many people answering phone calls and she can take care of any questions I may have. Note: This also happens with correspondence. At the top of some letters they give you a name to ask for when calling. I think they are all fictitious, you never get that person. Also, many times when you get correspondence, either it says to the effect: From: CY70 or it is signed CY70. Who is this? You never know.

Back to the story. I tell her I was told to call this number. She tells me to hold. Finally she comes back and says the call was to inform me that they rejected my offer of $800/mo. I told her that I was told that two weeks earlier. I told her I really was trying to handle the monthly payments directly between myself and the IRS. My employer is not very happy with the present setup. I then told her about the one person giving me a statute of limitations expiration date of 2004 and another saying it is now 2008. She checks and says that it was moved forward around 2000 when we ended the bankruptcy fiasco. Why then did their Appeals Office use a date of 2004? She didn't know. I told her about the $26,000 check and that mess, I told her about the garnishment She works in Collections and she/they knew nothing about these matters.

Around the end of November the bank told me that the funds that were frozen (approximately $30,000) would be sent to the IRS that day. About this time I also get a packet from the IRS. Inside are all my most recent appeal papers. I seems I forgot to sign the statement. I signed and returned all the forms.

In December 2004 I called the Nashville office to discuss the possibility of paying directly to the IRS. This would eliminate the involvement of my employer. I was told that based upon their records, I could do this. They would check into the matter. (Note: the people you talk to on the telephone are just conversationalists. They can't make decisions, they may give you their opinion, which is not always correct. I assume they mean well, but don't count on anything they tell you.) I was told to call back in two weeks.

I called back in mid-December, and was told that I couldn't pay direct since I had filed for bankruptcy in November of 2004. I told them I never did such a thing, or made such a filing. I asked their source of this information and demanded to speak to a Supervisor about this matter. No one knew anything except what they saw on their screen. They said they would look into the matter.

I was told that since I had no more liquid assets, (they took all my funds in October, 2004) I should file a new Offer In Compromise. The lady told me that she would send me the forms. I got the forms for the OIC in late December. I completed the forms and mailed them to a listed New York address. (Note: This is another problem. It is apparent to me that all these addresses have no data base networking capabilities.) This time, I also had to mail them $150.00, to cover their expenses.

As of the end of 2004 I had received no response to my October fax or my Appeal. Around March of 2005, I called to learn the status of my appeal from November 2004, and my OIC of 2005. I was told there would not be a decision for 6–9 months. In other words I continue to have my wages garnished until they reach a decision. If they rule in favor of my Appeal or accept my OIC (I really don't expect either), they will have received nine months of collections from me.

In May of 2005 my wife and her attorney go to the local IRS office and pay off the restaurant liability. Luckily, her attorney is with her since the woman at the counter has no intention of providing some type of receipt. The attorney demands such documentation.

Between the money paid against the restaurant liability, the $30,000 taken from my bank account and the wage garnishment, we will have paid nearly $150,000 to the IRS when the garnishment finally ends. This total was initially represented by a total sum of tax liabilities representing approximately $45,000. This number ($45,000) represents the combined original liabilities for Florida and the restaurant.

Finally, in June, 2005 I get the decision. Appeal and OIC denied. (Exhibit No.37) They state that their findings show that I am the party with sole responsibility to pay the monies due. This, in spite of the fact that I provided information that Florida Corp, acknowledged in the Bankruptcy Disclosure statement of 1992 that the corporation owed the funds to the IRS. It also stated the payment plan for such funds, and accepted the fact that if these funds were not paid per the schedule, the IRS could seize assets to cover the liability.

I am also told that I can not file another OIC, as I did. I only filed the second one because an agent suggested it, and sent me the forms! Finally, unless I want the statute of limitations to be extended even further into the future, it is suggested that I withdraw my OIC and Appeal. (Exhibit No 37).

I have recently hired a new attorney, one whom my wife has been using, she feels he is fair and honest. He advises that the withdrawal is probably the best move.

As long as I am employed, my wages will be garnished until August of 2007. That is approximately two years from now. If I die, am unable to work, or loose my employment for any reason, I have no idea what will happen.

Two months go by, July and August. In mid-September there is a letter in the daily mail-from the IRS. Now what? (Exhibit No. 39). In essence, what they are saying is that since I didn't pay my total bill due, they have the right to seize up to 15% of my social security funds. What would they do if I were not receiving social security payments? Until they started garnishing my wages I didn't need the social security money for daily living expenses. This money, and more from my salary income was being invested for the years when I could no longer work. At this point I see no alternative than to work to my dying day. I do note that the amount due has dropped to $33,000. Based upon what was paid to date I thought I still owed around $30,000. The extra $3,000 must be the yearly interest (10%). Also, with the wage garnishment, I will have paid a lot more than the $33,000 by the time the payments end. You have no way to fight this, you continue to pay and wait for the end. Note: There is another story relative to the interest and penalties, but you don't need that story at this time.

This letter comes from Kansas City. (This is the headquarters for collections). I hope you note how well acquainted I have become relative to various IRS offices, and the functions of such offices. I call the listed number. When I get a human voice, approximately ten minutes later, I repeat all the information I have already stated to the computer, just to get to that point.

"Yes, Mr. Meyer, we are looking at the possibility of withholding a portion of your social security funds since your appeal was never resolved". I asked her if she knew that they were already garnishing my wages. She had to check. She came back on the line and said, "Mr. Meyer, we show you are making payments (garnishment) but your case with the Appeals Office was never resolved." I told her it was resolved, and read her a portion of the letter I had received from the Appeals Office. (Exhibit No. 38). "Well," she said, "we didn't receive such information."

She then tells 'me' to call the Appeals Office and tell them to close my account and forward such information to the Kansas City office. I state to her," you work for the same agency (IRS), as the Appeals Office. Can you imagine their response to me, if I follow your instructions?" "Why don't you call them and resolve this matter directly with them?" "I can't make any outgoing calls, that is why you must call them" she states. Can you believe this? She also tells me to call her back in four days to verify that the Appeals Office sent them the information. At this point, steam is emanating from my ears!

I am to call the Appeals Office and give them instructions as to what they are to do with my account. These instructions will carry a very negative connotation. I agree with the action, but why must I, as the client, involve myself in an internal problem? You can be certain the Appeals Office is going to be real happy with me. In addition, when I call back to Collections, I will never get the same person with whom I had just spoken. Even if you are lucky enough to have recorded their name and ID number, the comment you get is, 'I have no idea if they are in the office at this time. We all can help you with your problem'. Right!

I call the Appeals Office. In this instance I do have a name, number and extension. I get the person who sent me the letter. Hallelujah! He sounds very reasonable, and says he remembers my case. I question that, but I explain the reason for the call, and what I was told to do (call him). He asks a few questions, and then said 'what is the woman's name (Collection Department) and ID number?' I told him I didn't have her name, but was able to get her ID number, which I gave to him.

Note: When you call any IRS office, and finally reach a human, the first response is: 'My name is Jane Doe and my ID number is 123—'. Unless you are aware of the response, you sit there and say to yourself, 'what did she say?'. Just as when you call a commercial organization, when they respond, you seldom understand the short greeting they give. They repeat this response so many times each day, when you hear it, it sounds like their mouth is filled with mush.

His response to me is "if you don't have a name, how can I contact her?" I repeated that I had her ID number, but there was no response. I also told him that she told me to call her back, and she certainly didn't insure that I had her name and ID number. Finally, he said he would look into the matter. He said something about new changes that had just gone into effect. He now had to work through Fresno, CA. He is located in Philadelphia, PA. I hung up the telephone.

The next day I come home and there is a message. I press the button. It is a woman from the IRS. It concerns my conversation with the Appeals Office. Again, I am given a name and direct number. She mentions she is in Fresno. I call, she answers the phone and acknowledges that she is the one who called me. This woman turns out to be the most personable IRS agent I have spoken to over these past fourteen years. I suspect she is fairly young, relative to tenure with the agency. She seems to be too interested in resolving a problem, she has not been 'automated' at this point, but that time regretfully, will come. My experience has shown me that at some point they all become essentially robots. They aimlessly repeat IRS policy, or give their opinion which is meaningless. They are very good at overwhelming you with forms and paperwork, or if they see they are nearing a situation which will require a decision on their part, they direct you to some other office.

As I make a broad examination of the people I have dealt with within the IRS, I reach the following conclusions:

1. The vast majority of government employees seek nothing but present and future personal security. They will do, and say, whatever they are told. If they

can't recall the 'agency' response to a question, they give you an ambiguous answer, or refer you to another office.

2. No one who seeks authority and responsibility enters government employment. Even if you are elevated to a 'managerial' position, the comments in conclusion No. 1 still apply. No one is going to be caught making a decision without some available opportunity to divert responsibility to someone else, or some other department. Responsibility for any potentially delicate decision is continually shuffled throughout departments and office locations. There are many examples of this activity throughout this narrative,

3. The last women I spoke of (Fresno location), represents something/someone I had never encountered in my fourteen year odyssey. First, she was spontaneous, straight forward, confident and self-assured. This is sooo different from anyone I encountered to date.

There is a need for 'lemming' types such as I have mentioned. I personally know people who worked for many years in the Federal government. Let me use the example of one of my brothers. Gordon spent four years in the USAF. He was trained as an intelligence analyst. The USAF sent him to a very well known university for two years to learn a foreign language. After the Air Force and college, he spent many years as an analyst for one of the government's top intelligence agencies.

Gordon didn't drink, smoke cheat on his wife or break any laws. For him, everything was 'by the book'. Although I have no way of knowing, I am sure he did a very fine job for the US government. However, and this is pure speculation, I'll bet he never went 'out on a limb', 'never pushed the envelope' and never 'stirred up the ranks'. I do know he didn't agree with many of the decisions made within his area, but he lived with them. Is this good or bad? Who am I to judge?

But you see, this is the same problem within the IRS. Ninety nine per cent of employees just want a job that pays reasonable wages and a very generous retirement. They will not question anything or anyone. They will certainly not speak for the 'client'. That is how you get into trouble with your supervisors. The last thing they want is for one of their people to create an issue they will rise above their management level.

They all want in, (a government job) and when their time is up, they all want out (retirement). No problems and a decent wage as they wait for retirement.

If 'clients' are hurt, improperly treated or abused with paperwork and indecision, that is the problem for someone else. They only do what they are told to do.

Now back to the agent in Fresno. First of all, she asked how I was doing. My response, "that depends on what you are going to tell me". "Well", she said, "I think you are in pretty good shape". She had talked to the Appeals Office and the Collections Office. They will drop any attempt to take any portion of my social security benefits. I appreciated hearing that, but then I asked her about when the statute of limitations ended. I figured that I should ask her for a formal opinion since I already had been given three different dates. I wanted to know when this burden would finally end. I told her about the letter from Appeals stating the garnishment would end in two years (2007). That would put me at seventy years of age!

She checked her files and said her records indicated 2008. She then said she would check with Appeals and call me back. She would also send me a letter documenting her answer. The 2008 date is in line with the date given to me by the local IRS office, but how can this be? I would think that the Appeals Office would certainly have the correct date (2007), since I would expect they review such information when making a decision. Again, who do you believe? Who is actually correct?

I recently dropped my attorney, at his recommendation, since everything seemed to be resolved. We both thought I would pay for two more years, and that would end it. I didn't like it, but I was finally ready to accept it. If I wanted to retain him again, it would mean several more thousands of dollars out of my pocket.

On October 18, 2005 I received a letter from the women in Fresno (Exhibit No. 40). In summary, it says the statute of limitations ends November 7, 2008. This is due to the fact that I filed an OIC and Appeals Process Hearing Request in early 2005. It turns out that whenever you file such forms, the statute of limitations is automatically extended.

Example, as of June 27, 2005, the statute of limitations was August, 2007. Even though I requested a termination of both procedures, as the Appeals Office had suggested, the statute of limitations was extended fifteen months between June 27 and August 30, 2005. The later date is when I received the letter acknowledging my request for termination.

For those of you who have never been in an adversarial position with the IRS, whenever you get the preliminary information, whatever the subject, you get approximately five or more pieces of correspondence explaining your rights. What you can do, how to go about exercising your rights and how you got into this situation. Nowhere on the forms (OIC and Appeals Process Hearing Request), which you must complete and submit, do they tell you that the statute of limitations will be extended if you file. I was told later that this information is within the 'supplemental information' which is mailed with the forms.

On October 21, 2005 I called the Appeals Office to speak to the person who sent me the letter with the August, 2007 date. It is immediately obvious that he has just spoken to the Fresno agent. The comments are one and the same.

I read him his letter stating that the statute of limitations is August, 2005. I read him the part that says if I withdraw the paperwork there will be no extension of the statute of limitations. What he tells me is that if I had not withdrawn the paperwork the statute of limitations would have been increased even further into the future. In other words, if you want to question, or debate any of their decisions you pay a price. There is an extended period of payment and you pay a fee to even file a rebuttal (remember I had to pay $150.00) just to file the OIC.

I mentioned how I had never requested an OIC form. I was sent to me by the IRS. I mentioned to him that an IRS agent suggested I file the second OIC and a request for an Appeals hearing. How can you (IRS) extend the statute of limitations on an OIC request you do not even accept? He apologizes for the confusion. That is easy to do. It's just a few words for him, for me it is fifteen additional months of payments on a bill I still feel is not my obligation.

As of this moment, I will try to work for three more years to pay this debt. I will be seventy-one. If I can do it, it's OK. My problem is, if I do manage to complete the garnishment, how will we live after that date?

Who is going to hire a seventy-one year old man? How do I know I will be able to do any type of meaningful labor? Right now, since starting anew to save for our 'later' lives, we could support ourselves for maybe three years.

There is an alternative.

Rick Meyer

# _Caption_
# EXHIBIT NO. 1

AUGUST, 1990

Recapitalization of Florida Corp.

Paragraph 6, Section (b), Portions i-iv.

This exhibit states that the President (myself) will not take any action without the consent of the Board, if the result would be to (i) incur any liability in excess of $5000. (iii) No payments inexceeding $5000. In summary, wilthout Board approval, I could not pay IRS obligations.

(iii)  There have been no changes in the financial condition, business or affairs of the Corporation since the date of the most recent period reflected in the Corporation's Financial Statements which would, in the aggregate, have a material effect on the business, properties, prospects, assets or financial condition of the Corporation.

(f) Stock Ownership.  The Shareholders own jointly 10 shares of the Corporation's voting common stock ($1.00 par value) (the "Shares"), representing, in the aggregate, all of the issued and outstanding shares of the Corporation.  All of the Shares are owned absolutely by the Sellers, free and clear of all liens, encumbrances and adverse claims.  There is no Shareholders' Agreement in effect which would restrict the transferability of the Shares.

(g) Agreements; Orders.  The Corporation is not subject to any writ, order, injunction, decree, award or judgment of any court, tribunal or governmental agency.

(h) Taxes.  The Corporation has timely filed all Federal, state and local tax returns which it is required to file and has no outstanding liability for any Federal, state or local taxes or interest or penalties thereon, whether disputed or not, except taxes not yet payable.

5.   Management of the Corporation After Recapitalization; Election of Directors.  Upon execution of this Agreement, the Shareholders of this Corporation shall hold a special meeting and shall vote their shares to elect the following as Directors of the Corporation to serve until the election of their successors or their prior death, removal, or resignation:

6.   Reduction in Number of Directors; Restrictions on President's Duties.  Concurrently with the execution of this Agreement, the Directors of the Corporation shall amend the Bylaws of the Corporation to provide as follows:

(a) The Corporation shall have five (5) directors:

(b) The President of the Corporation shall not, without the consent of a majority of the Board of Directors of the Corporation, have the power, or take any action, the result of which would be to:

(i) incur any liability or obligation in the name of or on behalf of the Corporation in excess of $5,000.00;

(ii) operate the plant leased by the Corporation other than on a full time, active basis;

(iii) make, or cause the Corporation to become a party to a contract or commitment, or renew, extend, amend, or modify any contract or commitment unless such contract or commitment is (a) entered into in the ordinary course of business; and (b) does not require payment of an aggregate amount in excess of $5,000.00;

(iv) make any capital expenditures or any capital additions or improvements requiring the payment of more than $5,000.00 for any one capital improvement, or an aggregate of more than $20,000.00 in any 12-month period for all capital additions and payments.

7.    Consent of Shareholders to Future Transactions.    As a material inducement to          to enter into the transaction contemplated by this Agreement, the Shareholders will, concurrently with the execution of this Agreement, execute an agreement, substantially in the form attached hereto as Exhibit "D", whereby the Shareholders agree to consent to and approve any future transactions that the Board of Directors may propose, provided that, if the transaction involves the sale or disposition of shares of stock of the Corporation to a person or corporation which is not a "related person", the Shareholders, if they so request, shall receive the same amounts received by the remaining shareholders for their shares.    For purposes of this Agreement, "related person" shall be defined to mean any parent or subsidiary of          , or any person or corporation directly owning a fifty percent (50%) or greater interest in

8.    Termination of Subchapter S Status.    The Corporation and          acknowledge and agree that the issuance of Stock of the Corporation to          will result in a termination of the Corporation's Subchapter S status under the Internal Revenue Code.    Accordingly, the Corporation's tax items for the year of the closing of the transaction contemplated by this Agreement shall be computed and allocated among the Shareholders on a pro rata basis, and          and the Shareholders agree to consent to elect the pro rata method for allocating the tax items.

9.    Default.    The occurrence of any of the following events shall constitute a default by the Corporation or the Shareholders (as applicable), under this Agreement:    (i) if the Corporation or the Shareholders fail or neglect to perform, keep or observe any covenant, condition, warranty or representation contained in this Agreement, or (ii) if any representation or warranty made by the

# *Caption*
# *EXHIBIT NO. 2*

SEPTEMBER 23, 1991

My letter of resignation. There were late payments made to the IRS in the past. They were paid, with penalty. Note that I stipulated that this transfer is only valid if Florida Corp. assumes all outstanding liabilities. At the time I didn't expect a response unless they would not accept my conditions.

Note: Later correspondence will show that Florida Corp. will acknowledge that they own 100% of the stock. In essence, indicating that they accepted my conditions for resigning, ie, assuming all liabilities of the corporation. The IRS had all this information.

ⓒ

*Casting For The Future*

President

September 23, 1991

Dear

 This letter is to confirm my resignation as President
of                        Inc., effective September 5, 1991.

 In addition, as we discussed on several prior dates, my
wife and I hereby transfer our remaining 25% ownership of
                  Inc. to        in return for the assumption
of all liabilities of                        Inc. by

Very truly yours,

# *Caption*
# *EXHIBIT No. 3*

Plan of Reorganization of Florida Corp.

October, 1992

Class II Priority Claims

1. The debtor (Florida Corp.) estimates the total outstanding taxes owed is approximately $119,000. Claimant is the IRS.

2. Debtor will make payments over 72 months. IRS shall retain its lien for a period of six years. If the debtor fails to make two consecutive payments, the claimant (IRS) is entitled to enforce the pre-petition claims.
Note: If the liabilities are not paid, the IRS can put a claim against the corporation assets. As time will show, the company made six payments (Approximately $17,000)) and then stopped payment. At that point the IRS came back after me.

This is a situation where the corporation acknowledged its obligation, and don't meet it. Instead of the IRS seizing assets, which is stated as a means of restitution in the Disclosure Statement, it backs away from Florida Corp. and comes after me. They (IRS) were aware of my resignation notice, my stipulation relative to corporate liabilities and the indirect acknowledgment of my terms by Florida Corp. when they state that they owned 100% of the corporate stock.

warranty claimants, may have the right to file administrative claims. If such claims are filed, the Debtor intends to deal with such claims by continuing to pay and perform on such claims in the ordinary course of the Debtor's business, and will not make any specific disbursement or performance on these claims at the time of Confirmation.

CLASS II --- <u>Priority Claims</u>

The Allowed Claims of this Class of Creditors may be impaired.

The Debtor believes that the following comprise all claimants who may be entitled to an allowance of a priority claim in accordance with Bankruptcy Code Section 507(a): (i) the United States Internal Revenue Service; (ii) The State of Florida, Department of Revenue; (iii) Florida Unemployment Compensation Fund; (iv)                            ; and (v) any other claimant riling and having an Allowed Claim under Section 507(a) of the Bankruptcy Code.

The Debtor estimates that the total amount of outstanding and unpaid priority taxes owed to these taxing authorities totals approximately $195,274.72, including the claim of the Internal Revenue Service in the approximate amount of $119,472.71.

The Debtor intends to treat all Allowed Priority Claims by making payments to these claimants over a seventy-two (72) month period with the first payment commencing one (1) year after the Consummation Date. The Debtor shall provide these Creditors with promissory notes in the amount of their Allowed Claim, which notes shall bear interest at 8.5% per annum and which shall amortize in equal monthly installments, inclusive of the interest rate set forth above, over seventy-two (72) months. All disbursements made to the Internal Revenue Service by the Debtor shall be applied first to the trust fund portion of any and all tax obligations. The Internal Revenue Service shall retain its statutory lien for a period of six (6) years from date of assessment of such lien. In the event the Debtor fails to make two consecutive payments called for hereunder, then this class of priority claimants shall be entitled to enforce their pre-petition claims as if no Chapter 11 proceeding had been filed and confirmed.

CLASS III --- <u>Creditor Holding Claim Secured by Personal Property</u>

The Allowed Claims of this Class of Creditors are unimpaired.

The Debtor has an unexpired executory contract with ' which holds a security interest in a serial number 401240, owned by the Debtor. Annexed hereto

(b)    Accountants employed by the Debtor and approved by the
       Bankruptcy Court to perform accounting work for the
       Debtor;

(c)    Appraisers and other expert witnesses if employed by the
       Debtor in connection with this Chapter 11 proceeding and
       confirmation of the Debtor's Plan of Reorganization; and

(d)    Any other administrative expenses allowed by the
       Bankruptcy Court pursuant to Section 503 of the
       Bankruptcy Code.

The Debtor shall pay all allowed administrative expenses
within ten (10) days after the Consummation Date of the Plan. The
Debtor is currently purchasing materials and supplies on credit
terms post-petition. These suppliers and vendors, as well as any
warranty claimants, may have the right to file administrative
claims. If such claims are filed, the Debtor intends to deal with
such claims by continuing to pay and perform on such claims in the
ordinary course of the Debtor's business, and will not make any
specific disbursement or performance on these claims at the time of
Confirmation.

Class II are Priority Claims. The Allowed Claims of this
Class of Creditors may be impaired.

The Debtor believes that the following comprise all claimants
who may be entitled to an allowance of a priority claim in
accordance with Bankruptcy Code Section 507(a): (i) the United
States Internal Revenue Service; (ii) The State of Florida,
Department of Revenue; (iii) Florida Unemployment Compensation

any difficulty in raising this cash.

### V. Current Officers and Directors and the Plan's Intention Respecting Officers and Directors

Officers and Directors of the Debtor shall maintain their positions with the Debtor. The Debtor believes that its officers, directors and management team, which have remained with the Debtor since inception and have been responsible for the Debtor's successful operation to date, are the best parties to guide the Debtor into the future. It should be reiterated that the Debtor's equity security holder shall retain its shares of stock in the Debtor but shall not receive any distribution or account on any such shares until all of the Debtor's Creditors have been paid in full under the terms and conditions of the Plan as embodied in the Confirmation Order.            terminated his position as the Debtor's president in March of 1991 and longer participates in the management or operation of the foundry business. Mr.

is presently the President of the Debtor and serves as a director but draws no salary from the Debtor. Mr.                    is an unpaid director of the Debtor and holds no officer position.

### VI. Contingencies

There are no contingencies to the confirmation of the Plan other than the Court entering the Confirmation Order confirming the Plan.

### VII. Hiring of Professional Persons/Functions

During the course of the Chapter 11 case, Debtor has hired                    to serve as its attorneys. The Debtor has also hired, as authorized by the Bankruptcy Court, the

# _Caption_
# _EXHIBIT No. 4_

Bankruptcy Disclosure Statement

Florida Corp. acknowledges the IRS obligation.

Section III (Page 10) states that Florida Corp. holds

100% of the common stock.

Note: If they own 100%, they must have accepted the conditions of my September 23, 1991 letter. I am not a lawyer (thank G0D), but how does Florida Corp. transfer stock ownership without a consent from the prior stockholder? The IRS had the same information I am sharing with you. They (IRS) do not pursue this matter, nor do they follow-up with action against Florida Corp. after receiving only six payments. It appears to me that there may be an issue of 'Professional Courtesy' between the IRS, Florida Corp. and their legal team.

to pay approximately $1,519.07 to such class of unsecured creditors within thirty (30) days of the Confirmation Date.

Class VI are Stockholder Claims. The Allowed Claims of all persons having a legal or equitable right to the ownership of stock of the Debtor shall retain their shares of stock in the Debtor but shall not receive any distribution or account on any such shares until all of the Debtor's Creditors have been paid in full under the terms and conditions of the Plan as embodied in the Confirmation Order.                                      a Florida corporation, holds one hundred (100%) of the issued and outstanding common shares in the Debtor.

### IV. Anticipated Means of Execution of Plan

In order to effect the execution of the Plan, the Debtor intends to continue its foundry operations and restricting its production activity to selected cast items which represent low-volume, high weight castings. These items have historically been profitable for the Debtor. With regard to payments to unsecured creditors, the Debtor shall use its cash flow from operations to make the payments to unsecured creditors called for hereunder. In the event additional funds are necessary to consummate the Plan, such funds will be provided by existing or new shareholders. Should the Debtor experience any temporary shortfalls and require additional infusions of cash during the term of the Plan, the Debtor anticipates that the amount needed to be contributed could be anywhere from $25,00 to $100,000. If the Debtor's projections of future operations are accurate, the Debtor does not anticipate any difficulty in raising this cash.

### V. Current Officers and Directors and the Plan's Intention Respecting Officers and Directors

Officers and Directors of the Debtor shall maintain their positions with the Debtor. The Debtor believes that its officers, directors and management team, which have remained with the Debtor since inception and have been responsible for the Debtor's successful operation to date, are the best parties to guide the Debtor into the future. It should be reiterated that the Debtor's equity security holder shall retain its shares of stock in the Debtor but shall not receive any distribution or account on any such shares until all of the Debtor's Creditors have been paid in full under the terms and conditions of the Plan as embodied in the Confirmation Order. Mr.                terminated his position as the Debtor's president in March of 1991 and longer participates in the management or operation of the foundry business. Mr. is presently the President of the Debtor and serves as a director but draws no salary from the Debtor. Mr.                is an unpaid director of the Debtor and holds no officer position.

### VI. Contingencies

There are no contingencies to the confirmation of the Plan other than the Court entering the Confirmation Order confirming the Plan.

### VII. Hiring of Professional Persons/Functions

During the course of the Chapter 11 case, Debtor has hired                , P.A. to serve as its attorneys. The Debtor has also hired, as authorized by the Bankruptcy Court, the

# <u>Caption</u>
## *EXHIBIT NO. 5*

June 10, 1993

This is a letter from the IRS stating that my protest for this obligation is rejected. They had all the information shown in the prior Exhibits. How can they reach such a conclusion? My rationalization is that they don't want to get involved. Go after the easiest mark.

Internal Revenue Service
District Director

Department of the Treasury

Date: 6/10/93

Employer Identification Number:

Name and Address of Corporation:

Tax Periods Ended:
    12/31/90 03/31/91
Kind of Tax:
    Form 941
Individual's Social Security Number:

Person to contact:

IRS Contact Telephone Number:

 

We have reviewed your protest dated 0/00/00, and determined that you are a responsible person in accordance with Section 6672 of the Internal Revenue Code, relating to liability of the corporation and periods shown above.

No new facts have been presented to alter that conclusion. The case will be reviewed and will then be forwarded to the Appeals Office for their consideration. You will be contacted for a hearing by an Appeals Officer at that time. If your name, address, or telephone number changes before you are notified of your hearing, please contact us with the changes so that there is no delay in your receipt of the hearing notice.

If you have any questions, please contact the person whose name and telephone number are shown above.

Sincerely yours,

*The company came out of nkrupt in April or May of '93 Acting Group Manager. Didn't this matter have to be resolved before this took place?*

Letter 1154(DO)   (Rev.4-89)

# <u>Caption</u>
## *EXHIBIT No. 6*

February 14, 1994

When I received the first notice from the IRS, I retained a local attorney.
This is a letter from my attorney asking me to come to his office. He
wanted to talk to an IRS agent relative to my Appeal.

LAW OFFICES

February 14, 1994

RE:                          - Internal Revenue Service
     Form

Dear

    I have received communication regarding our appeal from
    , an Appeals Officer of the Internal Revenue Service.
Would you please call my office to make an appointment to sign a
Waiver Extending Statutory Period for Assessment of the recovery of
the penalty.  In addition, I want you to spend some time with me
while we call Ms.         on the telephone to attempt to see if we
can resolve the matter.

    If you have any questions, please give me a call.

    Best regards.

                    Sincerely,

2/22 3PM

# <u>Caption</u>
## *EXHIBIT No. 7*

October 4, 1994

Letter from my attorney to the IRS. I rejected their settlement offer on a 50% basis. In hindsight, this was my worst decision. In my mind, it would be like pleading guilty, just to end the problem, even if you weren't guilty. I believe this now known as 'plea bargaining'.

At that time (and to this date), I didn't feel that I personally owed the money. At that time I had no knowledge of Offer in Compromise or the possibility of a payment plan. However, I made the decision.

LAW OFFICES

October 4, 1994

'LLM TAXATION

Internal Revenue Service
Philadelphia Appeals Office
701 Market Street
Suite 2200
Philadelphia, Pennsylvania 19106

Attention:
        Appeals Officer

RE:
    A:PHI:LM
    Trust Fund Recovery Tax
    Quarters Ending: 12/31/90 and 03/31/91

Dear

    I spoke to              last evening and he is both unwilling
and unable to agree upon a settlement at a fifty percent (50%)
basis.

    Best regards.

                        Sincerely,

cc:

# *Caption*
# *EXHIBIT No. 8*

October 25, 1994

A letter from my attorney giving his opinion and asking me what I wanted to do. He states that I have no confirmation that my September 23, 1991 letter was received, or accepted. Assume it was not received, and/or accepted. How did Florida Corp. get my 25% of the corporate stock? They never contacted me. The bankruptcy papers identify Florida Corp.. as having 100% ownership. How did they get that if they didn't contact me, or accept the conditions of my letter of resignation? The IRS had all this information. Didn't Florida Corp. have to prove their 100% ownership?

October 25, 1994

RE:  Letter to

Dear ·

    Your letter does indicate that .                        , Inc.
would continue to assume all liabilities of ·                  ,
Inc.  The only possible fly in the ointment or trying to assert
this letter is that apparently you do not have any confirmation in
writing from         responding to your letter.  I do believe that
we could make a fairly decent case for the continued requirement of
the  assumption  of  liabilities  since  your  resignation  was
conditioned upon the assumption of all liabilities.

    Please give me your instructions as to if and when you wish to
pursue    .                     , Inc.  I have not as yet heard from
the  attorney  in  Florida  relative  to  the  payments  under  the
reorganization plan.

    Best regards.

                            Sincerely,

Proceed

# _Caption_
# _EXHIBIT No. 9_

December 28, 1994

Letter from the IRS stating the same opinion they have given since the start
of this issue. I really wonder if anyone in the agency (IRS) actually looked
at any of the information listed earlier. It is my opinion they didn't, and
have no interest in doing so. As I look back, I feel my attorney failed me in
that he never put much credence in the evidence provided by the
aforementioned documents. Why should the IRS spend their time
examining these documents and possibly reaching a different conclusion?
They have someone's name (mine), and they will keep coming after me.

Internal Revenue Service

District Director

Department of the Treasury

P.O. Box 12051
Philadelphia, PA  19105

Person to Contact:

Telephone Number:

Refer Reply to:

Date:
December 28, 1994
Certified Mail Receipt#P 842 746 86(

Dear Mr. .    :

　　We have considered your claim for refund and abatement of a
Trust Fund Recovery Penalty in the amount of $40,089.81 assessed
against you as a responsible person in connection with the
failure of .                      ., to pay trust fund taxes
withheld from employees, for the period ending December 31, 1990
and January 31, 1991.

　　Our records reflect that the assessment was proper and made
on the basis of facts ascertained during our investigation of
　　　　　　　　　　　　　.  Your claim produced no information or
evidence to support a change in the original assessment.  This is
your legal notice that your claim is disallowed.

　　If you wish to bring suit or proceedings for the recovery of
any tax, penalties, or other moneys for which this disallowance
notice is issued, you may do so by filing such a suit with the
United States District Court having jurisdiction, or the United
States Court of Federal Claims.  The law permits you to do this
within two (2) years from the date of this letter.

　　If you have any questions, please contact the person whose
name and telephone number are shown above.

Sincerely yours,

Acting Chief, Advisory Unit

cc:　　　　　　　, Power of Attorney

# <u>Caption</u>
## *EXHIBIT NO. 10*

May 16, 1995

Letter from my attorney. He is telling me that what I told him about Florida Corp. making payments is correct. I had talked to the IRS in Florida to substantiate what I had learned from my contact within Florida Corp. My attorney notes that he told the IRS-Philadelphia about the payments being made in Florida. Why must I be the one to tell them? Why didn't they, IRS-Philadelphia know this? Personally, I think they did know it, they just refused to acknowledge it.

LAW OFFICES

OF COUNSEL

May 16, 1995

'LLM TAXATION

Pennsylvania

**Re:  Tax Liability**

Dear

You are correct that Philadelphia is handling the matter, but as you recall, we refused their offer to settle for 50%, thus allowing the collection process to continue. I wrote a letter to them advising them of what was transpiring in Florida, ie. the fact that Florida was receiving monies from the bankruptcy reorganization to satisfy the tax liability. That fact in and of itself does not stop the Internal Revenue Service from seeking collection from you, but I am hoping that as time passes and the liability reduces, they will forbear attempting to collect from you and thus, allow the corporation to pay off the liability.

If you have any questions regarding the foregoing, please let me know.

Best regards.

Sincerely,

# <u>Caption</u>
# *EXHIBIT NO. 11*

June 19, 1995

A letter from the IRS-Philadelphia. Just 30 days earlier (Exhibit No. 10),
my attorney notified this office that the Florida Corp. was paying as
scheduled. I personally gave him this information. The payments started
January 17, 1995. Does anyone with the IRS know what is happening?
The IRS acknowledged to me that I didn't have to pay as long as Florida
was paying. Note the signature to this letter from the IRS. There is none!

001119

** IF YOU HAVE ANY QUESTIONS, **
** REFER TO THIS INFORMATION: **
NUMBER OF THIS NOTICE:
DATE OF THIS NOTICE:   06-19-‚⌐
TAXPAYER IDENT. NUM:
TAX FORM:
TAX PERIOD:   03-31-91

Department of the Treasury
Internal Revenue Service
PHILADELPHIA, PA   19255

FOR ASSISTANCE CALL:          215-574-9900 LOCAL PHILA.
                              1-800-829-1040 OTHER PA

              WE INTEND TO LEVY - RESPOND NOW
      * * * THE AMOUNT YOU OWE IS $42,062.35.        * * *
      - (AVOID ADDITIONAL INTEREST: PAY THIS AMOUNT IN FULL IN 10 DAYS.)

     THIS IS A FORMAL NOTICE OF OUR INTENT TO LEVY (SEIZE) YOUR
PROPERTY, OR THE RIGHTS TO IT, TO PAY THE TAX YOU OWE.  WE
PREVIOUSLY SENT YOU NOTICES REQUESTING THE FULL AMOUNT YOU OWE FOR
THIS OVERDUE TAX, BUT HAVE YET TO RECEIVE IT.

     The $42,062.35 you owe includes penalty and interest computed
to the date of this notice.  If we receive your full payment by
06-29-95, we will stop penalty and interest charges.  Otherwise, we
will continue to charge additional penalties and interest until the
amount you owe is completely paid.

     Send your full payment to us today.  Make your check or money
order for the amount you owe payable to the Internal Revenue Service.
Write your social security number or employer identification number
on your payment.  Tear off the payment voucher stub from the end
of this notice and send it with your payment in the enclosed
envelope.

     If we don't receive your full payment by 07-19-95, we may levy
your property without further notice to you.  This means the law
allows us to take your property or rights to property such as real
estate and personal property (for example, automobiles and business
assets) to collect the amount you will owe on your tax account shown
on the front page of this letter.  We may also take your wages,
bank accounts, commissions and other income.  We have enclosed
Publication 594, Understanding the Collection Process, which gives
you additional information.

     We may file a Notice of Federal Tax Lien at any time to protect
the government's interest.  A lien is a public notice to your
creditors that the government has a right to the interest in
your property, including property you acquire after we file the
lien.  When there is a lien on your property, it may be difficult
for you to obtain credit in the future or sell your property.

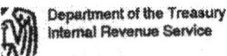

Department of the Treasury
Internal Revenue Service

```
NUMBER OF THIS NOTICE:
DATE OF THIS NOTICE:    06-19-95
TAXPAYER IDENT. NUM:
TAX FORM:
TAX PERIOD:    03-31-91
```

is late up to a maximum of 25% of the unpaid tax.

The federal income tax is a "pay-as-you-go" tax. You must pay the tax as you earn or receive income during the year. There are two easy ways to do this:

1.  WITHHOLDING: If you are an employee, your employer will withhold income tax from your pay. Tax is also withheld from other types of income -- including pensions, bonuses, commissions, and gambling winnings. In each case, the amount withheld is paid to the Internal Revenue Service in your name.

If too little tax is being withheld from your wages to pay the taxes you will owe at the end of the year, you should file a new Form W-4, Employee's Withholding Allowance Certificate, with your employer to change the amount of withholding.

2.  ESTIMATED TAX PAYMENTS: If you don't pay your tax through withholding, or don't pay enough tax through withholding, you have to estimate the tax you will owe and make payments during the year directly to the IRS.

If you need more information about changing your Form W-4 or making estimated tax payments, please call us today. Publication 505 explains both methods in detail. You may request forms and Publication 505 by calling 1-800-829-FORM.

If you write to us or send additional information (including Form 9465, Installment Agreement Request), use the IRS address on the first page of this notice. Be sure to include your telephone number, the best time for us to call, and any necessary changes to our record of your name and address.

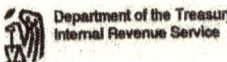
**Department of the Treasury**
**Internal Revenue Service**

NUMBER OF THIS NOTICE:
DATE OF THIS NOTICE:   06-19-95
TAXPAYER IDENT. NUM:
TAX FORM:
TAX PERIOD:   03-31-91

We don't want to take the actions described above.  In fact, we prefer that you call us at the telephone number(s) that are shown on the front page of this notice to make arrangements to pay your taxes voluntarily.  By working with us to resolve your tax problem, you can help us avoid the lien and levy actions outlined in this notice.  However, if we don't hear from you, we will have no choice but to take these collection actions.

If you can't pay the amount you owe now, CALL US IMMEDIATELY at the number(s) shown on the first page of this notice.  We want to help you resolve this bill -- don't delay!

If you think this bill is incorrect, or you want to know how we arrived at the amount you owe, CALL US at the number(s) on the first page of this notice and we can tell you.

If you believe that we didn't apply a payment you made to your account for this tax period, CALL US at the phone number(s) on the first page of this notice.  When you call, have the following payment information available:

(1)   IF YOU DEPOSITED THE PAYMENT DIRECTLY WITH THE IRS -
- a copy of the front and back of your canceled check;
- your money order receipt, the name and address of the issuing station with the amount and date of purchase; or
- the cash amount, date, and number on the cashier's receipt.

-- OR --

(2)   IF YOU DEPOSITED THE PAYMENT WITH A BANK -
- the deposit amount, the date of the deposit, and the name and address of the bank where you made the deposit.

THE AMOUNT YOU OWE IS $42,062.35.
We figured this amount by adding:

| | |
|---|---|
| Amount unpaid from prior notices | $39,989.81 |
| Late payment penalty | $0.00 |
| Interest | $2,072.54 |

The amount unpaid from prior notices may include tax, penalties, and interest you still owe IRS.  It also should reflect any credits and payments we received from you since the last notice we sent you.

As of the date of this notice, the late payment penalty increases to 1% of the unpaid tax for each month or part of a month the payment

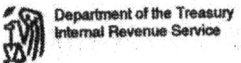

Department of the Treasury
Internal Revenue Service

NUMBER OF THIS NOTICE:
DATE OF THIS NOTICE:     06-19-95
TAXPAYER IDENT. NUM:
TAX FORM:
TAX PERIOD:   03-31-91

We don't want to take the actions described above.  In fact, we prefer that you call us at the telephone number(s) that are shown on the front page of this notice to make arrangements to pay your taxes voluntarily.  By working with us to resolve your tax problem, you can help us avoid the lien and levy actions outlined in this notice.  However, if we don't hear from you, we will have no choice but to take these collection actions.

If you can't pay the amount you owe now, CALL US IMMEDIATELY at the number(s) shown on the first page of this notice.  We want to help you resolve this bill -- don't delay!

If you think this bill is incorrect, or you want to know how we arrived at the amount you owe, CALL US at the number(s) on the first page of this notice and we can tell you.

If you believe that we didn't apply a payment you made to your account for this tax period, CALL US at the phone number(s) on the first page of this notice.  When you call, have the following payment information available:

    (1)  IF YOU DEPOSITED THE PAYMENT DIRECTLY WITH THE IRS -
          - a copy of the front and back of your canceled check;
          - your money order receipt, the name and address of the
            issuing station with the amount and date of purchase; or
          - the cash amount, date, and number on the cashier's
            receipt.

              -- OR --

    (2)  IF YOU DEPOSITED THE PAYMENT WITH A BANK -
          - the deposit amount, the date of the deposit, and the
            name and address of the bank where you made the deposit.

THE AMOUNT YOU OWE IS $42,062.35.
We figured this amount by adding:

| | |
|---|---:|
| Amount unpaid from prior notices | $39,989.81 |
| Late payment penalty | $0.00 |
| Interest | $2,072.54 |

The amount unpaid from prior notices may include tax, penalties, and interest you still owe IRS.  It also should reflect any credits and payments we received from you since the last notice we sent you.

As of the date of this notice, the late payment penalty increases to 1% of the unpaid tax for each month or part of a month the payment

001119

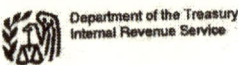 Department of the Treasury
Internal Revenue Service

NUMBER OF THIS NOTICE:
DATE OF THIS NOTICE:  06-19-95
TAXPAYER IDENT. NUM:
TAX FORM:
TAX PERIOD:  03-31-91

_____

══════

KEEP THE PAGE(S) ABOVE FOR YOUR RECORDS          DETACH BELOW
--------------------------------------------------------------------
Send this PAYMENT VOUCHER with your payment in the enclosed
envelope.
                                    ACR
                                                        9523
                    Number of this notice:
                    Date of this notice: 06-19-95 9529
        Taxpayer Identifying Number:
                        Form                    Tax Period 03-31-91

                    AMOUNT YOU OWE.. $42,062.35
                    Subtract any payments you
                    believe we haven't credited
                    --------------------------
                        PAY THIS AMOUNT..

# <u>Caption</u>
## *EXHIBIT NO. 12*

June 25, 1995

My response to the June 19th letter.

To: IRS-Philadelphia


Re: (          (6-19-95)
T.I.N.
Form

June 25.1995

I must tell you, whoever you are–since nobody signs these notices, I just don,t understand the thinking or the true purpose of your continual efforts to collect these monies from me.

The money is due the U.S. Government–no question. However:

1. You have been notified several times through my attorney (Mr.                    ) that       has an approved payment plan for these monies. Approved by the Florida Bankruptcy Court and the Tampa office of the I.R.S.

2.         officials have told me that approximately $25,000 has been paid on this liability. You have never confirmed or denied if this is true. I have received no comment at all from your office.

3. Irregardless of the amount paid to date by         , if your Tampa office approved the payment plan for these funds, why do you continually harass me for the same payments?

Are you prohibited from contacting the Tampa office to see if the payments have been made? In fact–are you aware of the payment plan? If not–why not?

It appears to me that you are more interested in harassing me than you are in recovery of this money. In addition–I am told that the Tampa office has ceased all efforts to recover the monies from Mr.         and Mr.         as long as the payment schedule is met. Why am I not included in this cessation of action to collect from individuals? Why do you discriminate against me?

In an effort to put some rationality into this situation, I request the following information.

What is the remaining balance? If .      has not met the payment schedule, why hasn't the IRS taken the company to recover these funds?

In the past you have indicated that .      has primary responsibility and Messrs .       . and myself have secondary obligations. You treat me as if I am the only one obligated. You indicate that you are oblivious to the actions taking place in Tampa. Are you uninformed? If so-Why? Or , do you know what is happening-but refuse to acknowledge it, or inform me.

I would truly like to get this matter resolved. It is taking its toll on myself and my marriage. Is it too much to be treated the same as the gentlemen in Florida? Do you really care who pays , as long as you get the money? A response will be greatly appreciated.

# _Caption_
# _EXHIBIT NO. 13_

July 17, 1995

My June letter is being sent to Jacksonville by the Philadelphia office. Finally, a signature on the IRS correspondence. All files were supposedly sent to the Philadelphia office, but my letter is being sent back to Florida since they are more familiar with the case!

PROBLEM RESOLUTION OFFICE
INTERNAL REVENUE SERVICE
P.O. BOX 6073
PHILADELPHIA, PA     19114

Date:

JULY 17, 1995

Re: Your Inquiry Dated

JUNE 25, 1995

DEAR MR _____

WE ARE NOTIFYING YOU THAT YOUR INQUIRY DATED JUNE 25, 1995 HAS BEEN TRANSFERRED TO THE JACKSONVILLE DISTRICT OFFICE WHICH OVERSEES THE TAMPA OFFICE YOU INDICATED IN YOUR LETTER.

SINCE THEY ARE MORE FAMILIAR WITH THE SITUATION, THEY WILL BETTER ANSWER YOUR INQUIRY.

YOU WILL BE CONTACTED BY THEM, YOU NEED NOT MAKE OTHER INQUIRIES UNTIL THEN.

IF YOU HAVE ANY FURTHER QUESTIONS PLEASE CALL _____ AT _____ *

WE APOLOGIZE FOR ANY INCONVENIENCES.

Your Telephone Number:

( )

SINCERELY

Best Time to Call During Normal
Working Hours:

Title:

TAX EXAMINER

Employee No.: _____

* NOT TOLL FREE.

Form 5260-A (Rev. 7-87)

# _Caption_
# _EXHIBIT NO. 14_

August 14, 1995

Letter from Jacksonville, Florida. They will leave me alone, for the time being, since Florida Corp. is paying on the liability. Note that they (IRS) state that if there is a default, they will proceed with collection action against responsible individuals. Later action indicates that is referencing to me alone. This is in light of the fact that Florida Corp. indicated in the Bankruptcy Filing that they accepted the fact that the IRS could seize their assets if they failed to pay the obligation.
Again, why didn't the IRS follow through and get the funds from Florida Corp., who apparently had the wherewithal to pay the obligation?

Internal Revenue Service

**Department of the Treasury**

District
Director

P. O. Box 35045, Jacksonville, FL 32202

Person to Contact:

Telephone Number:

Refer Reply to:

Date:

**AUG 14 1995**

*Must check with*
*Phil Special*
*Procedures off*
*Mrs.*
*every bmo to insure*
*is paying*
*Request no action*

*Bankruptcy Advisor*
*checks m*

*147*

Re:

Dear Mr. :

This is in response to your correspondence dated June 25, 1995,
and referred to our Problem Resolution Office.  Your request
concerned ceasing collection actions on the Trust Fund Recovery
Penalty  (TFRP) assessed against  you for tax periods ending
March 31, 1991, and December 31, 1991.  We apologize for the
delay in our response.

We are pleased to grant your request.  No further collection
action regarding the TFRP is being taken.  We understand that
payments are being made by                          However,
if                    , which is currently in Chapter 11
bankruptcy, defaults on their payment plan, the Internal Revenue
Service will immediately proceed with collection actions against
responsible  individuals without  prior  notification  from  our
Collection Division.

We apologize for the problems encountered and hope we have been
of assistance.

Sincerely yours,

*Must do this every*
*bmo since I live in*
*PA & Jacksonville can*
*not handle Phil area.*

Problem Resolution Officer

There is no correspondence from August 14, 1995 to January 6, 1997.

# _Caption_
# _EXHIBIT NO. 15_

January 6, 1997

Final Notice! The amount is now $48,225. The note is from IRS-Philadelphia. They have no idea, or knowledge, that Florida Corp. had paid on the debt. If you will note, (Exhibit No. 14) states two different tax periods. March 1991 and December, 1991. I resigned on September 23, 1991. The bankruptcy papers say I resigned March, 1991. Therefore I have no liability for the December, 1991 taxes. Examine the January 6, 1997 note. The identified period is March, 1991. What happened to the December, 1991 liability?

Department of the Treasury
Internal Revenue Service
PHILADELPHIA, PA 19255

Notice Number:
Notice Date:      01-06-97
SSN/EIN:
Caller ID:

G

IₐIₐIₐIₐIIₐₐIIIₐIIₐₐₐIₐₐIₐₐₐIₐIIIₐₐₐₐIₐIIₐIIₐIIₐIIII

## Final Notice !!

### We intend to levy. Please respond NOW.

(To avoid additional penalty and interest, pay your overdue tax in full today.)

Our records indicate you have not paid your overdue tax. The law requires that you pay your tax at the time you file your return. This is formal notice of our intent to <u>levy</u> (take) your paycheck, bank account, auto or other property if we do not receive your payment in full. We can also file a Notice of Federal Tax Lien, if we have not already done so.

### PAY YOUR TAX TODAY
### Account Summary

| Form: | Tax Period: 03-31-91 |
|---|---|
| Prior Balance: | $39,989.81 |
| Last Payment: | $0.00 |
| Penalty to date: | $0.00 |
| Interest to date: | $8,265.85 |
| **New Balance:** | **$48,255.66** |

See enclosed Publication 594 that explains
your rights and responsibilities as a taxpayer.

Questions? Call us at  1-800-829-8815

---

Please mail this part with your payment, payable to Internal Revenue Service

Notice Number: CP
Notice Date:    01-06-97

*write on your check:*

| 03-31-91 | |

Amount Due:
          $48,255.66

Internal Revenue Service
PHILADELPHIA, PA 19255

# <u>Caption</u>
# *EXHIBIT NO. 16*

January 18, 1997

My response to January 6th note. You can't imagine how frustrating it is to be hounded by people who have no knowledge of the complete picture. Why is that? Is it my obligation and responsibility to keep the IRS informed? Can't they, or are they not allowed to communicate with each other?

To: IRS-Philadelphia
Re: (        (1-6-97)
SSN:

*Letters generated.*

Jan. 18, 1997

Approximately one week ago I received a registered letter from your office (         ).
Since that time, I have made at least four calls to your office ( 1-800-829-8815) in an
attempt to find out what this is all about.

I have no idea what is behind this notice, since any information that I receive on this
matter must be gained by my own initiative.  Your wording: FINAL NOTICE
We intend to levy
PAY YOUR TAX TODAY
infer that I have failed in my obligation to your agency.  New Balance: $48,255.66.  This
is the initial amount due when this episode began more than three years ago.

During that time I had to spend a significant amount of my money on legal fees in an
effort to defend myself and clarify the situation.  It was only after I wrote a letter informing
your office that the firm in question (                       ) in Florida was making
payments on this obligation.  My continual question was;  Why continue to come after me
for the money, if the company was making the payments on a schedule approved by your
agency?  Also, why maintain this effort to collect all the monies from me if the company
had and was paying on the total due?

This problem involves a corporation                              ) and three
individuals: myself,                  and                       . I turned the company over to the
two gentlemen with the stipulation that they assume all       ' liabilities.  Obviously they
have not , and this is my problem to resolve.

After I sent you the above referenced letter, I received a response from your Problem
Resolution Office.  In this letter it was acknowledged that           was making payments as
required by a court approved plan permitting        to return from bankruptcy.  I assume the
IRS approved this plan as a primary creditor of the company.  I was also told that your
agency reviews these payments every six months and if there was a lapse in payments I
would be notified.  I assume this means that the company and the other two gentlemen
would also be notified.  The date of this letter was Aug. 14, 1995

Based on the above information, how can $48,000 still be owed if you agency
acknowledged timely receipt of payments.?  Based upon what I was told by the Problem
Resolution people, payments must have been made up to approximately 6/96.  If so, again,
how can the original amount still be due?

I am just a pawn in this matter-which I accept.  Messrs.         and         are in Florida and control all actions by the company.  After receiving this latest notice, I did some investigation and have been told that                         no longer exits and is now operating under a new name.  Is this permitted by bankruptcy courts and due creditors such as you agency unless the obligations of the prior company have been settled?

I am so sick of this problem, I don't know where to turn.  Before I do anything more, please provide me with the payment history from.         .  I would like to know exactly where the remaining amount of the obligation lies.

# <u>Caption</u>
## *EXHIBIT NO. 17*

February 7, 1997

IRS-Philadelphia response to my January 18th letter. We will look into the matter.

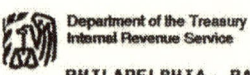

Department of the Treasury
Internal Revenue Service

PHILADELPHIA, PA    19255

In reply refer to:
Feb. 07, 1997  LTR

Input Op:

Taxpayer Identification Number:

Dear Taxpayer:

We are handling your inquiry of Jan. 18, 1997, in our Problem
Resolution Program, which corrects problems that have not been
resolved through regular Internal Revenue Service contacts.  We
understand your problem involves the following:
civil penalty balance due.

We will contact you by Feb. 28, 1997, to provide you with an update.
Meanwhile, please let us know if you change your address or phone
number.  Also let us know if your problem changes or if you hear
anything else from the IRS.

If you have questions, please contact
between the hours of 5:00 pm and 11:00 pm Monday through
Friday at .            .  If you are not in the local calling area,
there may be a charge for this call.  If you prefer, you may write
to us at:

                    Problem Resolution Office
                    Internal Revenue Service
                    Attention:
                    PO Box
                    Phila.,PA

Whether you call or write, please give us your telephone number and
tell us the best time to call.  We are sorry for the inconvenience
this problem has caused you and thank you for your patience and
cooperation.

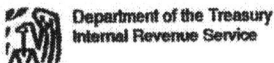

Department of the Treasury
Internal Revenue Service

Feb. 07, 1997

Input Op:

Sincerely yours,

PROBLEM RESOLUTION OFFICER

# _Caption_
# _EXHIBIT NO. 18_

April 28, 1997

Final Notice!! Two months after the IRS tells me they will be back to me by February 28, 1997, I get this notice. I never got the promised reply. Three months after their prior 'Final Notice'. The amount is now $1500 higher.

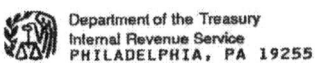

Department of the Treasury
Internal Revenue Service
PHILADELPHIA, PA 19255

Notice Number:
Notice Date:      04-28-97
SSN/EIN:
Caller ID:

Illdlollodlltllluddololuddlll.....ldlll.ll.ll.llll

# Final Notice !!

## We intend to levy. Please respond NOW.

(To avoid additional penalty and interest, pay your overdue tax in full today.)

Our records indicate you have not paid your overdue tax. The law requires that you pay your tax at the time you file your return. This is formal notice of our intent to levy (take) your paycheck, bank account, auto or other property if we do not receive your payment in full. We can also file a Notice of Federal Tax Lien, if we have not already done so.

### PAY YOUR TAX TODAY
### Account Summary

| Form: CIVPEN | Tax Period: 03-31-91 |
|---|---|
| Prior Balance: | $39,989.81 |
| Last Payment: | $0.00 |
| Penalty to date: | $0.00 |
| Interest to date: | $9,616.90 |
| **New Balance:** | **$49,606.71** |

See enclosed Publication 594 that explains
your rights and responsibilities as a taxpayer.

Questions? Call us at

# *Caption*
## *EXHIBIT NO. 19*

May 19, 1997

I send a letter explaining my predicament to Senator William Roth
(Delaware). I know he is looking at IRS practices. I supplied a detailed
summary of all correspondence I had sent and received from the IRS.
There was no response. None was expected.

Senator William V. Roth
104 Hart Senate Office Building
Washington, D.C. 20510

May 19, 1997

Dear Senator Roth:

Through various news reports, I am aware that your committee is looking into various issues relative to the Internal Revenue Service. I have been living a nightmare for the past six years due to the actions of this agency, which I find impossible to comprehend.

I agree that the agency is owed money by a company I owned at one time. My issue is the means by which they harass, stonewall and just plan ignore my questions and attempts to resolve this matter.

Enclosed is a summary of some of the correspondence that has been exchanged over this six year period. Wouldn't a rationale question be, 'Why isn't this issue resolved after six years?'. As I stated earlier, the money is due to the government. I trust that after you have read the enclosures you may have some understanding of my despair. In my opinion, they have attempted to isolate me from any actions that have occurred, relative to this company (.      ) and continually feed me notices that state I owe them the total amount, plus interest. Even though I know that a significant amount of the money has been paid.

The enclosures can not due justice to the continual pressure on me, and my frustration in knowing what has been happening relative to payment, but not being able to get the IRS to acknowledge anything. If this case is of interest to you, I will gladly visit one of your offices in Delaware to provide more details of this continuing dilemma.

Very truly yours,

# <u>Caption</u>
# *EXHIBIT NO. 20*

June 6, 1997

This is in response to my January 18th letter. They date it February 18, 1997. Note also that they date the tax period as 1993. The writer also lists the tax period as January 31, 1991, within the text of the letter. What happened to December, 1991?

Internal Revenue Service          **Department of the Treasury**
Problem Resolution Office         **P.O. Box 12090, Phila., PA  19105**

Date: June 6, 1997               PERSON TO CONTACT:
                                 TELEPHONE NUMBER: (
                                 HOURS: 8:00 a.m. - 4:00 p.m.
                                 FAX NUMBER:
                                 TIN: .
                                 TAX FORM(S): Civil Penalty
                                 TAX PERIOD(s): 1993

Dear Mr.

This is in further response to your inquiry to the Problem
Resolution Office dated February 18, 1997.

Under the Trust Fund Recovery provisions, any officer or employee
determined responsible for the non-payment of tax may be
personally liable for the income tax withheld from employees'
checks and the employee's portion of FICA.  Our records indicate
that you were the only officer of
and therefore the only individual assessed a civil penalty for
the corporation's Employer's Quarterly Tax Return, for the period
ending January 31, 1991.

Enclosed is copy of payment information you requested.  Penalty
and interest will continue to accrue until the account becomes
full paid.

If you have any questions about how we resolved the problem, or
if you receive further correspondence, please contact the person
whose name, telephone number and hours are shown above.
Depending on your location, there may be a long distance charge.
If you prefer to write, direct your letter to the above address.

Please let us know your telephone number and the hours you may be
reached by phone.

We are sorry for any inconvenience and delay you have
experienced.

                                 Sincerely yours,


                                 PRP Caseworker

Enclosure

# *Caption*
# *EXHIBIT NO. 21*

June 13, 1997

This is a Transaction Sheet which shows amount due and payments received. On October, 1992 Florida Corp. stated they would pay the tax obligation over the next seventy-two months. The seventy-two month period would end October, 1998. The Transaction Sheet shows that the first payment was made on January, 17,1995. Three months later. They made a total of seven payments, approximately $17,000. Note at the bottom of the form it states 'as of November 16, 1993 (one year after the Plan of reorganization) there wiould be no legal action pending'.
This statement is made before any payments have been made!
What is this?

PAGE NO-0001

DATE REQUESTED 06-12-97

FORM NUMBER: 941

IRS EMPLOYEE

PRINT DATE 06-13-97

TAX PERIOD: DEC 1990

TAXPAYER IDENTIFICATION NUMBER:

--- ANY MINUS BELOW SIGNIFIES A CREDIT AMOUNT ---

| | | |
|---|---|---|
| ACCOUNT BALANCE: | 14,863.41 | |
| ACCRUED INTEREST: | 18,757.43 | AS OF 06-23-97 |
| ACCRUED PENALTY: | 6,462.76 | AS OF 06-23-97 |
| ACCOUNT BALANCE PLUS ACCRUALS: | 40,083.60 | |
| TAX PER TAXPAYER: | 27,501.10 | |

02-15-91 RETURN DUE DATE OR RETURN RECEIVED DATE (WHICHEVER IS LATER)
04-01-91 PROCESSING DATE

TRANSACTIONS

| CODE | EXPLANATION | DATE | MONEY AMOUNT (IF APPLICABLE) |
|---|---|---|---|
| 150 | RETURN FILED AND TAX ASSESSED | 04-01-91 | 27,501.10 |
| 166 | LATE FILING PENALTY | 01-31-91 | 1,237.55 |
| 186 | DEPOSIT PENALTY | 04-01-91 | 1,375.06 |
| 276 | PENALTY FOR LATE PAYMENT OF TAX | 04-01-91 | 412.52 |
| 196 | INTEREST ASSESSED | 04-01-91 | 523.50 |
| 360 | FEES & COLLECTION COSTS | 10-14-91 | 12.00 |
| 670 | SUBSEQUENT PAYMENT | 09-24-91 | 0.00 |
| 582 | LIEN | 09-27-91 | |
| 520 | BANKRUPTCY SUIT PENDING | 04-21-92 | |
| 520 | BANKRUPTCY SUIT PENDING | 04-21-92 | |
| 670 | SUBSEQUENT PAYMENT | 01-17-95 | 2,362.95- |
| 670 | SUBSEQUENT PAYMENT | 02-09-95 | 2,362.95- |
| 538 | DECREASE TRUST FUND TAX-RELATED 100% PENALTY PD | 12-28-94 | 100.00- |
| 670 | SUBSEQUENT PAYMENT | 08-30-95 | 2,292.70- |
| 670 | SUBSEQUENT PAYMENT | 10-25-95 | 2,292.70- |
| 670 | SUBSEQUENT PAYMENT | 02-22-96 | 2,292.70- |
| 670 | SUBSEQUENT PAYMENT | 03-29-96 | 2,247.16- |
| 670 | SUBSEQUENT PAYMENT | 04-25-96 | 2,247.16- |
| 521 | LEGAL SUIT NO LONGER PENDING | 11-16-93 | |

There is no further correspondence between June 13, 1997 and

and August 26,2002

# <u>Caption</u>
# *EXHIBIT NO. 22*

August 26, 2002

Final Notice-Intent to levy. Amount is now $62,000. An Appeal
form is enclosed. I file an Appeal.

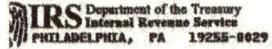

**IRS** Department of the Treasury
Internal Revenue Service
PHILADELPHIA, PA   19255-0029

Notice Number: 
Notice Date:  AUG. 26, 2002
Social Security Number:

---

Collection Assistance:

---

## FINAL NOTICE
## NOTICE OF INTENT TO LEVY AND NOTICE OF YOUR RIGHT TO A HEARING
### *PLEASE RESPOND IMMEDIATELY*

We previously asked you to pay the federal tax shown on the next page, but we haven't received your payment. This correspondence is your notice of our intent to levy under Internal Revenue Code (IRC) Section 6331 and your right to receive Appeals consideration under IRC Section 6330.

We may also file a Notice of Federal Tax Lien at any time to protect the government's interest. A lien is a public notice to your creditors that the government has a right to your current assets, including any assets you acquire after we file the lien.

If you don't pay the amount you owe, make alternative arrangements to pay, or request Appeals consideration within 30 days from the date of this letter, we may take your property, or rights to property. Property includes real estate, automobiles, business assets, bank accounts, wages, commissions, social security benefits, and other income. We've enclosed Publication 594 with more information, Publication 1660 explaining your right to appeal, and Form 12153 to request a Collection Due Process hearing with Appeals.

TO PREVENT COLLECTION ACTION, PLEASE SEND YOUR FULL PAYMENT TODAY

- ☐ Make your check or money order payable to United States Treasury.
- ☐ Write your social security number on your payment.
- ☐ Send your payment and the attached payment stub to us in the enclosed envelope. The amount you owe is shown on the next page.

If you have recently paid this tax or you can't pay it, call us immediately at the telephone number shown at the top of this letter and let us know.

The assessed balance may include tax, penalties, and interest you still owe. It also includes any credits and payments we've received since we sent our last notice to you.

Enclosures:
Copy of this letter
Pub 594
Pub 1660
Form 12153
Envelope

CP 90 (Rev. 02-2002)

## ACCOUNT INFORMATION

| Form Number | Tax Period | Assessed Balance | Statutory Additions | Amount You Owe |
|---|---|---|---|---|
| CVL PEN | MAR. 31, 1991 | $29,754.81 | $32,278.36 | $62,033.17 |

**Payment Stub**                    Fold and return this page with your request, inquiry, or payment.

Your Telephone Number:              Best Time to Call

(   )_____-_____                _____ AM _____ PM

Amount you owe:       $62,033.17
Less payments not
included
Adjusted amount

Internal Revenue Service
PHILADELPHIA, PA   19255-0029

# _Caption_
## _EXHIBIT NO. 23_

September 3, 2002

I sent a letter to the IRS. I propose a payment plan.

To: Internal Revenue Service

September 3.2002

Based upon my best recollection, the last correspondence I received on this issue was 1997. Five years ago. I also know from direct conversation with your Florida office that they had assigned a 'Unable to Pay' or some similar designation to this case. The only reason your office is involved is due to the actions of a very inept attorney who had been recommended to me. I still don't agree that I owe the money. I submitted a legal document covering this subject. During a telephone conversation with someone in your office, an immediate decision was made that it had no effect on the issue.

Your correspondence says you have asked me to pay, but you have not received the money. I could not pay in 1992, or whenever this issue began, and I regret to tell you that if anything, my situation is much worse now. I just can't comprehend what assets people must have to be able to pay the $30K amount , much less the $62K.

In 1998 my wife and I filed for bankruptcy. Your agency has a copy of the Discharge. At that point we lost all assets/equity that we had hoped to use for our retirement. Since then I have been working for $14.00/hr. just to live a minimal life. In a few days I will turn 65, and hope to continue with my present job. My wife has been on disability for the past 2 years. If I loose my job I will have to get some minimum wage type position since there is no way we can live on SS and DIS. My job has some very physical aspects to it, and my employer is dramatically cutting manpower costs. In essence, I have got to work until I drop over dead, or enter a nursing home under Medicaid.

We filed Collection Information Statement with you office in 1999. We never had any response. Now, we get this notice. I received my first SS check in mid-August for .
    I plan to save the majority of this for when I can't work. I have spent 8 years of Hell trying to fight this issue. You send me a notice. I respond . Several years later another notice and my response. I give up. What do you want from me? I am not going to accept your threatening notices-do what you will

Based upon my

| | |
|---|---|
| SS Part A for two | 120 |
| SS Supp for two | 270 |
| Present prescription and miscell med. cost | 150 |

Pre Tax remainder

I estimate that we need at least $2500/mo. to live at a very minimal standard. This means that I must work at least 40/wk at $6.00/hr. To meet our needs. Who knows how long I can work?

MY hope is to save my SS money until I loose my present job/income. At that point I will still need to find other employment, but at least we will have some investment income and a small amount of funds for emergencies.

I can't afford it, but I am willing to make some type of minimum payment (over time) if it will end this nightmare.

## <u>Caption</u>
## *EXHIBIT No. 24*

September 3, 2002

I file the Appeal. I must admit I am very short with my comments.

# Request for a Collection Due Process Hearing

Use this form to request a hearing with the IRS Office of Appeals only when you receive a **Notice of Federal Tax Lien Filing & Your Right To A Hearing Under IRC 6320**, a **Final Notice - Notice Of Intent to Levy & Your Notice Of a Right To A Hearing**, or a **Notice of Jeopardy Levy and Right of Appeal**. Complete this form and send it to the address shown on your lien or levy notice for expeditious handling. Include a copy of your lien or levy notice(s) to ensure proper handling of your request.

*(Print)* Taxpayer Name(s):_____

*(Print)* Address: _____

Daytime Telephone Number:_____    Type of Tax/Tax Form Number(s):_____

Taxable Period(s):_____

Social Security Number/Employer Identification Number(s):_____

Check the IRS action(s) that you do not agree with. Provide specific reasons why you don't agree. If you believe that your spouse or former spouse should be responsible for all or a portion of the tax liability from your tax return, check here [__] and attach Form 8857, Request for Innocent Spouse Relief, to this request.

_____ **Filed Notice of Federal Tax Lien  (Explain why you don't agree. Use extra sheets if necessary.)**

_✓_ **Notice of Levy/Seizure (Explain why you don't agree. Use extra sheets if necessary.)**

1. Don't owe
2. Don't have money

I/we understand that the statutory period of limitations for collection is suspended during the Collection Due Process Hearing and any subsequent judicial review.

Taxpayer's or Authorized Representative's Signature and Date:_____    9-3-02

Taxpayer's or Authorized Representative's Signature and Date:_____

IRS Use Only:

IRS Employee *(Print)*: _____    IRS Received Date:_____

Employee Telephone Number: _____

Form **12153** (01-1999)    Catalog Number 26685D

**(Over)**    Department of the Treasury - Internal Revenue Service

# <u>Caption</u>
# *EXHIBIT NO. 25*

February, 2003

In early 2003 I receive the paperwork for an Offer in Compromise. I didn't solicit these forms, in fact, I didn't know what it was until I read the information. I completed the paperwork and submitted the forms on March 14, 2003. In summary, it is a proposal on my part to seek settlement for a sum which is less than the amount which the IRS is attempting to collect.

**IRS**

Department of the Treasury
Internal Revenue Service
www.irs.gov
Form 656 (Rev. 5-2001)
Catalog Number 16728N

**Form 656**

# Offer in Compromise

**IRS RECEIVED DATE**

Item 1 — Taxpayer's Name and Home or Business Address

Name

Name

Street Address

City                          State      ZIP Code

Mailing Address (if different from above)

Street Address                                         **DATE RETURNED**

City                          State      ZIP Code

---

**Item 2 — Social Security Numbers**

(a) Primary

(b) Secondary

**Item 3 — Employer Identification Number (included in offer)**

(a)

(b)

**Item 4 — Other Employer Identification Numbers (not included in offer)**

**Item 5 — To: Commissioner of Internal Revenue Service**

I/We (includes all types of taxpayers) submit this offer to compromise the tax liabilities plus any interest, penalties, additions to tax, and additional amounts required by law (tax liability) for the tax type and period marked below: (Please mark an "X" in the box for the correct description and fill-in the correct tax period(s), adding additional periods if needed).

☐ 1040/1120 Income Tax — Year(s)

☒ 941 Employer's Quarterly Federal Tax Return — Quarterly period(s) (a) 12/31/96  —  3/31/91
(b) 2/31/97  —  8/31/98

☐ 940 Employer's Annual Federal Unemployment (FUTA) Tax Return — Year(s)

☐ Trust Fund Recovery Penalty as a responsible person of (enter corporation name)

for failure to pay withholding and Federal Insurance Contributions Act Taxes (Social Security taxes), for period(s) ending

☐ Other Federal Tax(es) [specify type(s) and period(s)]

Note: If you need more space, see another sheet titled "Attachment to Form 656 Dated_____." Sign and date the attachment following the listing of the tax periods.

**Item 6 — I/We submit this offer for the reason(s) checked below:**

☒ Doubt as to Liability — "I do not believe I owe this amount." You must include a detailed explanation of the reason(s) why you believe you do not owe the tax in Item 9.

☒ Doubt as to Collectibility — "I have insufficient assets and income to pay the full amount." You must include a complete Collection Information Statement, Form 433-A and/or Form 433-B.

☐ Effective Tax Administration — "I owe this amount and have sufficient assets to pay the full amount, but due to my exceptional circumstances, requiring full payment would cause an economic hardship or would be unfair and inequitable." You must include a complete Collection Information Statement, Form 433-A and/or Form 433B and complete Item 9.

**Item 7**

I/We offer to pay $ 4800.00  (must be more than zero). Complete Item 10 to explain where you will obtain the funds to make this offer.

Check one of the following:

☒ Cash Offer (Offered amount will be paid in 90 days or less.)

Balance to be paid in: ☐ 10; ☐ 30; ☐ 60; or ☐ 90 days from written notice of acceptance of the offer.

☐ Short-Term Deferred Payment Offer (Offered amount will be paid in MORE than 90 days but within 24 months from written notice of acceptance of the offer.)

$_____ within _____ days (not more than 90 — See Instructions Section, Determine Your Payment Terms) from written notice of acceptance of the offer; and

beginning in the _____ month after written notice of acceptance of the offer, $_____ on the _____ day of each month for a total of _____ months. (Cannot extend more than 24 months from written notice of acceptance of the offer.)

☐ Deferred Payment Offer (Offered amount will be paid over the life of the collection statute.)

$_____ within _____ days (not more than 90 — See Instructions Section, Determine Your Payment Terms) from written notice of acceptance of the offer; and

beginning in the first month after written notice of acceptance of the offer, $_____ on the _____ day of each month for a total of _____ months.

NOTE: Signature(s) of taxpayer required on last page of Form 656

Item 10:

I am offering an amount of $4000.00
It will come from our assets.

We can't survive unless I find a job. This payment will only speed up that time at which we go into a negative cash flow position.

I'll find some way, do whatever I must to take care of myself and my wife.

Please accept the offer so we can get this 10 year mental/financial burden off of our backs.

# _Caption_
## _EXHIBIT NO. 26_

July 30, 2003

This is in response to my Appeal filed September 3, 2002. Ten months later! At a point in the future, I come to the conclusion that this gentleman is the most honest, relative to giving me straight answers, than anyone in the entire organization. This correspondence dealt with the possible request for additional information, none was requested.

**Internal Revenue Service**
Appeals Office
701 Market Street

Philadelphia PA

Date:  July 30, 2003

**Department of the Treasury**

**Person to Contact:**

Employee ID Number:
Tel:
Fax:
**Refer Reply to:**
AP:
In Re:
Due Process - Levy
**Tax Period(s) Ended:**
03/1991

This letter is our acknowledgement that we received your case for consideration in our Philadelphia Appeals Office on March 31, 2003.

In this letter we will explain who we are, what we do, how we do it, who you can talk to, and what you can expect.

Who We Are, What We Do, and How We Review Your Case
Appeals is separate from - and independent of - the division of the Internal Revenue Service proposing the action you disagree with.  What we do is review and resolve disputes. We do this in a fair and impartial manner by using the law and judicial decisions to weigh the facts.  We conduct our reviews by:  (1) telephone, (2) mail, and/or (3) personal interviews.

What You Can Expect
We will make every attempt to contact you as quickly as possible.  You can expect the "Person to Contact" listed above to consider the facts in your case and try to resolve the dispute.  This person may also ask for additional information to specifically explain or support the information in your file.

If our office determines that you owe the IRS, the law requires a charge for interest until you pay the amount you owe in full.

What You Can Do
• Respond quickly if asked to send additional information,
• If you wish to stop or reduce interest on part or all of the proposed balance due, you can make payments to the address listed above toward the tax or post a cash bond,
• Contact the "Person to Contact" listed above with any questions about the appeals process or how you can prepare for your hearing, and
• Research our website at www.irs.gov/appeals for more information.

Sincerely,

Appeals Officer

## <u>Caption</u>
## *EXHIBIT NO 27*

August 5, 2003

I receive a request for more information. I must complete Form 433.
This is basically a financial statement. I had earlier completed such a form.
Another example of one IRS office having no idea of what another office is
doing. I forwarded the forms, identified as Exhibit No. 25.

Internal Revenue Service
Appeals Office

Philadelphia PA

Date: August 5, 2003

Department of the Treasury

**Person to Contact:**

  Employee ID Number:
  Tel:
  Fax:
  **Refer Reply to:**

  **In Re:**
    Due Process - Levy
  **Social Security or Employer
  Identification Number:**

  **Tax Period(s) Ended:**
  03/1991

8-4:30

### We Received Your Request for A Collection Due Process Hearing
### And We Need More Information

I've received your request for a Collection Due Process Hearing. If you would like me to consider alternative methods of collection such as an Offer in Compromise or an Installment Agreement, you must provide me with the items below.

- A completed Collection Information Statement (Form 433-A for individuals and/or Form 433-B for businesses. I've enclosed the forms for your convenience).

Please send me the items above within 30 days from the date of this letter. I cannot consider certain collection alternatives in your hearing without the requested items. I will contact you after that date to schedule a hearing. I've enclosed a return envelope for your convenience.

Please contact me with any questions or concerns you might have regarding my request or the Collection Due Process procedure itself. You'll find my telephone number listed above.

Sincerely,

Appeals Officer

# *Caption*
# *EXHIBIT NO 28*

May 21,2004

My Appeal is denied.

**Internal Revenue Service**

Philadelphia, PA

Date: **MAY 2 1 2004**

Mike

**201**

**Certified Mail**

**Department of the Treasury**

**Person to Contact:**

   Employee ID Number:
   Tel:
   Fax:
   Refer Reply to:

**Tax Type/Form Number:**
   Misc. Penalty/MFT 55
**In Re:**
   Collection Due Process Hearing
   (District Court)
**Tax Period(s) Ended:**
   03/1991

**NOTICE OF DETERMINATION**
**CONCERNING COLLECTION ACTION(S) UNDER SECTION 6320 and/or 6330**

Dear Mr.

We have reviewed the taken or proposed collection action for the period(s) shown above. This letter is your Notice of Determination, as required by law. A summary of our determination is stated below. The attached statement shows, in detail, the matters we considered at your Appeals hearing and our conclusions.

If you want to dispute this determination in court, you have 30 days from the date of this letter to file a complaint in the appropriate United States District Court for a redetermination.

The time limit for filing your complaint (30 days) is fixed by law. The courts cannot consider your appeal if you file late. If the court determines that you made your complaint to the wrong court, you will have 30 days after such determination to file with the correct court.

If you do not file a complaint with the court within 30 days from the date of this letter, your case will be returned to the originating IRS office for action consistent with the determination summarized below and described on the attached page(s).

If you have any questions, please contact the person whose name and telephone number are shown above.

**Summary of Determination**

*? Unilateral!*

It is determined that there is no doubt as to your liability. You do not have the ability to make an installment agreement and your OIC for $ 4000.00 is inadequate as you have the ability to pay more than the offered amount. Compliance is sustained.

*? based on what?*

Sincerely,


Appeals Team Manager


cc: Attachment to - **Letter 3194, Notice of Determination**
See attached sheet

# *Caption*
# *EXHIBIT NO. 29*

June 29, 2004

My OIC is denied. Refer to the sheet 'Balancing Effective Collection and Intrusiveness'. I speak to a gentleman in the Appeals Office. He said the statute of limitations ended December, 2004. At this point they (IRS) will take all my liquid assets since I can not be obligated to a payment plan extending beyond December, 2004.

**Internal Revenue Service**
Appeals Office

Philadelphia, PA ¡

Date: **JUN 2 9 2004**

**Department of the Treasury**

**Person to Contact:**

Employee ID Number
Tel:
Fax:
**Refer Reply to:**

**In Re:**
Offer in Compromise
**Tax Period(s) Ended:**
1991/03 and 1997/06 through 1998/06

Dea

This refers to your offer of $4,000.00, submitted March 14, 2003 to compromise your liability for the tax period(s) ending 1991/03 and 1997/06 through 1998/06.

We are sorry, but your offer is rejected because the tax is held to be legally due and an amount larger than the offer appears to be collectible. We do not have authority to accept an offer in these circumstances.

We must therefore ask you to pay your account in full as soon as possible. If you have any questions, please contact the person whose name and telephone number are shown above.

                                Sincerely,




                                Appeals Team Manager

Enclosures:

ATTACHMENT TO LETTER 3194


COLLECTION DUE PROCESS - LEVY


| Taxpayer | Type of Tax | Period(s) |
|---|---|---|
| | Trust Fund Recovery Penalty | 1991/03 |


MATTERS CONSIDERED AT THE APPEALS HEARING

### Applicable Law and Administrative Procedures

With the best information available, the requirements of various applicable law or administrative procedures have been met.

IRC Section 6331(d) requires that the Service notify a taxpayer at least 30 days before a Notice of Levy can be issued. Transcripts show that this notice was mailed to you.

IRC Section 6330(a) provides that no levy may be made unless the Service notifies a taxpayer of the opportunity for a hearing with Appeals. A FINAL NOTICE - NOTICE OF INTENTION TO LEVY AND YOUR RIGHT TO A HEARING was sent to you by certified mail on 08/26/2002. You filed your appeal on 09/04/2002, less than 30 days after Form 1058 was issued.

You were given the opportunity to raise any relevant issue relating to the unpaid tax or the proposed levy at the hearing in accordance with IRC Section 6330(c). You raised the same issue as you have previously risen in Appeals and the Trust Fund Recovery Penalty was again sustained.

This Appeals Officer has had no prior involvement with respect to these liabilities either in Appeals or Compliance.

what does this mean?

### Balancing Efficient Collection and Intrusiveness

You are not eligible for an Installment Agreement because of your inability to pay within the Statute of Limitations. You have filed an Offer in Compromise but this is being rejected because the Offer in Compromise is for $ 4,000.00 and your liquid assets are approximately $ 27,000.00 according to your statements.

You state that you are 67 years old and need the assets for living expenses and cannot make them available for an amended Offer in Compromise. Therefore, Compliance is sustained.

# <u>Caption</u>
# *EXHIBIT NO. 30*

July 19, 2004

I receive this hand written note from the local IRS office. I am to re-submit Form 433, liquidate my assets and make payment for that amount.

**Department of the Treasury**
**Internal Revenue Service**

Date:

7/9/04

Re: Your inquiry dated

_____

Taxpayer identification number:

_____

Tax period:

1991

Dear Mr

A review of your information shows you have liquidable assets to pay down the debt.

$16627  Portfolio IRA
2978   Portfolio Equity.
4178

Please redo the 433A and/or liquidate the assets to make payment.

Signature

Title:     IRR            28

Employee number

# <u>Caption</u>

## *EXHIBIT NO. 31*

August 5, 2004

My letter to the local IRS. I had talked to an agent by telephone. She called me. You never can get anyone to answer your call. You may get a recording telling you to leave a message. She now wants all liquid assets plus $1650/month for forty months. The Appeals Office had said all they wanted was the assets and no payments after December, 2004.

Subject: Enclosed

August 5,2004

I regret I can not locate the fax number you gave me, so I am sending this through the postal system.

1. Letter from Mr.          . Note he references 1991 and 1998. I also have a listing which states the 1991 obligation at $29,754.81.This correspondence is dated 5/19/04. I don't understand how one part of your agency can give me such a number, while your number is more than double this amount ($1650/mo for 40 months). I also have a computer printout from a Florida office that lists the due amount at $18,158. This is dated 6-13-97. Even if I use 10% interest, it doubles the amount (7 yr.) but that is still a long way from $66,000.

   I await the form 433A. I have no idea how to complete the form for 1991, and another copy for 1997/98. Unless you offer comments with the form, I will do my best for meaningful completion.

## Caption
## *EXHIBIT No. 32*

Local office gives me a new date for the statute of limitations.

**Department of the Treasury**
**Internal Revenue Service**

Date:

_G/14/04_

Taxpayer Identification Number

Tax Period

_941   ACCTS_

Dear:
    Enclosed are current transcripts as of 9/15/04 and total balance due calculations as of 10/1/04.
    I have sent the 433 A + B forms for review and will advise.
    The Statute of Limitations for the civil penalty is currently 2/29/08.
    The balances change daily based on accrued penalty + interest amounts.

Telephone Number          Best time to call during normal working hours

(    )

_Mrs._

Signature

                                        _TRR_

Employee Number          Title

Catalog Number 42403P          Form 5260 (Rev. 2-2002)
                                        www.irs.gov
☆ U.S. GOVERNMENT PRINTING OFFICE: 2002—750-518     _5.1_

## <u>Caption</u>
## *EXHIBIT No. 33*

September 22, 2004

I am asked to submit a new OIC or a payment plan.

Department of the Treasury
**Internal Revenue Service**

Date:

9/22/04

Taxpayer Identification Number

1991.

Tax Period

Mr.

I am sending you the Form 652 offer in compromise and the Form 9465 Installment agreement. Please decide which route you would like to take. I will hold the forms you sent me until I receive either one.

Please use the balance listed on the calculation I recently sent you for the debt under your Social Security number.

Telephone Number    _ Best time to call during normal working hours

Mrs.

Signature

Employee Number          Title          TRR

Catalog Number 42403P          Form 5260 (Rev. 2-2002)

☆ U.S. GOVERNMENT PRINTING OFFICE: 2002—760-518          www.irs.gov

32

# <u>Caption</u>

# *EXHIBIT NO. 34*

October 11, 2004

My letter to the local IRS. I submit a check to pay the obligation owed on the restaurant. As I explain in the letter, I don't know who to beleive relative to my Florida obligation. In addition, the Appeals Office said the statute of limitations expired at the end of the year. The local office is now telling me it is February 29, 2008. Who do I beleive? I decide I will put the money on the restaurant account. At least we can settle that matter. The IRS doesn't like this action, as you will read later.

To: Internal Revenue Service

From

SSN:

Oct.11, 2004

Re:

1.

Enclosed is a check for $24,900. Check Number: 1486. This check is to be deposited against the liability for the                                    . This information is also shown on the check. This amount is the sum of all "Tax Per Taxpayer" for the 5 quarters related to this issue. 6-9-12/97 to 3-6/98.

I hope, and trust, this matter will now be resolved.

I am submitting everything I have been saving for my retirement years. I just turned 67. My employer recently asked me about my future plans. That means 'when are you leaving?' I can't afford to leave. Who can live on ,          from Soc. Sec?

I agree that I owe this money to the government. I have no idea if the numbers you gave me are correct, and I have to intention to go back to any old records that I may have and try to validate them. What I give you, is what I got.

I have several reasons for putting my money against the .          account. Number 1, I never felt I was liable for the          account. I will give rationale later in this note. I won't trouble you with the details, since it is meaningless, relative to the decision of the IRS. Number 2, I don't know how to be diplomatic about this, but either I can't interpret data given to me, or IRS offices operate mutually exclusive of each other, ie, one office has no idea what activities go on at another, relative to one particular account.

I have summary sheets for 3/91 dated 8/12/04 and 9/15/04. Both cover the periods 11/01/94 to 8/22/04. The period in question is 3/91 -8/23/04. Was there no activity from 3/91 to 11/94? Enclosed is an activity sheet from your Jacksonville office dated 6/13/97. This sheet shows payments of $14,600 to this account. Your sheets cover this period, but show no payments. In summary, all this is moot. I have given you all I have. I am normally a fighter when I think I am right. There is no opportunity to fight your agency unless you have unlimited resources. All I have left is tentative employment, a home with little equity, a wife with severe arthritis and a very short employment period ahead of me.

From your viewpoint, this scenario is a daily routine. For me, and anyone else in this situation, this is a once in a lifetime position. It is very emotional. To the IRS , personal feelings are immaterial, this is not true for an individual on the other side of the case.

Note: You recently sent me forms relative to a payment plan, and OIC. I still offer my check as payment for the                          . The OIC route is strictly a one way opportunity for the IRS. I already tried that path. The payment plan is essentially a formal way to pay my way into retirement poverty. Instead of saving what I can for when I am forced to retire, give the funds to you. Then when I must retire I have nothing but Soc. Sec.

Enclosed is my check to cover the liability for the ·

Note:  Please forward a receipt/acknowledgement of the sum paid against account

# <u>Caption</u>
# *EXHIBIT NO. 35*

October 16, 2004

I receive multiple correspondence from the IRS. Philadelphia, Pittsburgh, and Kansas City.

1. Federal Tax Lien on our residence.
2. Wage Levy (Garnishment) on my wages.
3. Freeze my bank account.

**IRS** Department of the Treasury
Internal Revenue Service       **CERTIFIED MAIL**
1001 LIBERTY AVE - SUITE 1300
PITTSBURGH, PA 15222

Letter Date: 10/12/2004
Taxpayer Identification Number:

Person to Contact:
P S LANE
Contact Identification Number:

Contact Telephone Number:

N~
JS
PL I
fox:

## Notice of Federal Tax Lien Filing and Your Right to a Hearing Under IRC 6320

We filed a Notice of Federal Tax Lien on 10/05/2004 because our records show the following:

| Type of Tax | Tax Period | Amount Owed |
|---|---|---|
| | 03/31/1991 | 29629.81 |

The lien attaches to all property you currently own and to all property you may acquire in the future. It may also damage your credit rating and hinder your ability to obtain additional credit.

You have a right to request a hearing with us to appeal this collection action and to discuss your payment method options. *To explain the different collection appeal procedures available to you, we've enclosed Publication 1660, Collection Appeal Rights.*

If you want to request a hearing, please complete the enclosed form 12153, *Request for a Collection Due Process Hearing,* and mail it to:

Internal Revenue Service

PO Box
KANSAS CITY, MO

You must request your hearing by   11/12/2004.

We'll issue a Certificate of Release of the Federal Tax Lien within 30 days after you pay the full amount owed. To get your current balance, contact the person whose name and telephone number appear at the top of this letter.

(over)

Letter 3172 (DO) rev. (11-20

| Form 668 (Y)(c) | Department of the Treasury - Internal Revenue Service |
|---|---|
| (Rev. February 2004) | **Notice of Federal Tax Lien** |

| Area: WAGE & INVESTMENT AREA #2 | Serial Number | For Optional Use by Recording Office |
|---|---|---|
| Lien Unit Phone: | | • This Notice of Federal Tax Lien has been filed as a matter of public record. |

As provided by section 6321, 6322, and 6323 of the Internal Revenue Code, we are giving a notice that taxes (including interest and penalties) have been assessed against the following-named taxpayer. We have made a demand for payment of this liability, but it remains unpaid. Therefore, there is a lien in favor of the United States on all property and rights to property belonging to this taxpayer for the amount of these taxes, and additional penalties, interest, and costs that may accrue.

- IRS will continue to charge penalty and interest until you satisfy the amount you owe.
- Contact the Area Office Collection Function for information on the amount you must pay before we can release this lien.
- See the back of this page for an explanation of your Administrative Appeal rights.

Name of Taxpayer

Residence

**IMPORTANT RELEASE INFORMATION:** For each assessment listed below, unless notice of the lien is refiled by the date given in column (e), this notice shall, on the day following such date, operate as a certificate of release as defined in IRC 6325(a).

| Kind of Tax (a) | Tax Period Ending (b) | Identifying Number (c) | Date of Assessment (d) | Last Day for Refiling (e) | Unpaid Balance of Assessment (f) |
|---|---|---|---|---|---|
| | 03/31/1991 | | 08/23/2004 | 09/22/2014 | 29629.81 |

Place of Filing

Total    29629.81

This notice was prepared and signed at ____PHILADELPHIA, PA____ , on this,

the _30th_ day of _September_ , _2004_ .

| Signature | Title |
|---|---|
| for P S LANE | 12-00-0000 |

(**NOTE:** Certificate of officer authorized by law to take acknowledgment is not essential to the validity of Notice of Federal Tax Lien Rev. Rul. 71-466, 1971 - 2 C.B. 409)

Part 3 - Taxpayer's Copy

CAT. NO 60025X
Form **668** (Y)(c) (Rev. 02-04)

| (Rev. January 2001) | | Notice of Levy on Wages, Salary, and Other Income | | | | |

DATE: 10/02/2004

IRS ADDRESS·

KANSAS CITY, MO

TO:   P

TELEPHONE NUMBER
OF IRS OFFICE:
TOLL FREE

NAME AND ADDRESS OF TAXPAYER:

IDENTIFYING NUMBER(S):

| Kind of Tax | Tax Period Ended | Unpaid Balance of Assessment | Statutory Additions | Total |
|---|---|---|---|---|
| CIVPEN | 03-31-1991 | $    29,629.81 | $    39,162.83 | $    68,792.64 |
| | | | Total Amount Due ▶ | $    68,792.64 |

We figured the interest and late payment penalty to _____ 11-02-2004 _____ .

Although we have told you to pay the amount you owe, it is still not paid.

This is your copy of a Notice of Levy we have sent to collect this unpaid amount. We will send other levies if we don't get enough with this one.

This levy requires the person who received it to turn over to us: (1) your wages and salary that have been earned but not paid yet, as well as wages and salary you earn in the future until this levy is released, and (2) your other income that the person has now or is obligated to pay you. These are levied to the extent they are not exempt as explained on the back of Part 5 of this form.

If you decide to pay the amount you owe now, please **bring a guaranteed payment (cash, cashier's check,** certified check, or money order) to the nearest IRS office with this form, so we can tell the person who received this levy not to send us your money. If you mail your payment instead of bringing it to us, we may not have time to stop the person who received this levy from sending us your money.

If you have any questions, or want to arrange payment before other levies are issued, please call or write us. If you write to us, please include your telephone number and the best time to call.

**Please see the back of Part 5 for instructions.**

| Signature of Service Representative | Title **Operations Manager, Collection** |

DATE:    10/02/2004

REPLY TO:

*Bid 10/22*

TELEPHONE NUMBER
OF IRS OFFICE:
TOLL FREE

KANSAS CITY, MI

P

TO:

IDENTIFYING NUMBER(S):

| Kind of Tax | Tax Period Ended | Unpaid Balance of Assessment | Statutory Additions | Total |
|---|---|---|---|---|
| CIVPEN | 03-31-1991 | $ 29,629.81 | $ 39,162.83 | $ 68,792.64 |

THIS LEVY WON'T ATTACH FUNDS IN IRAs, SELF-EMPLOYED INDIVIDUAL RETIREMENT PLANS, OR ANY OTHER RETIREMENT PLANS IN YOUR POSSESSION OR CONTROL, UNLESS IT IS SIGNED IN THE BLOCK TO THE RIGHT.

Total Amount Due ▶   $ 68,792.64

We figured the interest and late payment penalty to      11-02-2004

Although we have told you to pay the amount you owe, it is still not paid. This is your copy of a notice of levy we have sent to collect this unpaid amount. We will send other levies if we do not get enough with this one.

Banks, credit unions, saving and loans, and similar institutions described in section 408(n) of the Internal Revenue Code must hold your money for 21 calendar days before sending it to us. They must include the interest you earn during that time. Anyone else we send a levy to must turn over your money, property, credits, etc. that they have (or are already obligated for) when they would have paid you.

If you decide to pay the amount you owe now, please bring a guaranteed payment (cash, cashier's check, certified check, or money order ) to the nearest IRS office with this form, so we can tell the person who received this levy not to send us your money. If you mail your payment instead of bringing it to us, we may not have time to stop the person who received this levy from sending us your money.

If we have erroneously levied your bank account, we may reimburse you for the fees your bank charged you for handling the levy. You must file a claim with the IRS on Form 8546 within one year after the fees are charged.

If you have any questions, or want to arrange payment before other levies are issued, please call or write us. If you write to us, please include your telephone number and the best time to call.

Signature of Service Representative

Title

**Operations Manager, Collection**

FORM 8519 (Rev. 01-01) 895160

(Rev. January 2001)

## Notice of Levy

DATE: 10/02/2004

REPLY TO:

TELEPHONE NUMBER
OF IRS OFFICE:
**TOLL FREE**

KANSAS CITY, MO

NAME AND ADDRESS OF TAXPAYER:

TO:

IDENTIFYING NUMBER(S):

| Kind of Tax | Tax Period Ended | Unpaid Balance of Assessment | Statutory Additions | Total |
|---|---|---|---|---|
| CIVPEN | 03-31-1991 | $ 29,629.81 | $ 39,162.83 | $ 68,792.64 |

THIS LEVY WON'T ATTACH FUNDS IN IRAs, SELF-EMPLOYED INDIVIDUALS' RETIREMENT PLANS, OR ANY OTHER RETIREMENT PLANS IN YOUR POSSESSION OR CONTROL, UNLESS IT IS SIGNED IN THE BLOCK TO THE RIGHT. ———➤

Total Amount Due ➤ $ 68,792.64

We figured the interest and late payment penalty to_____ 11-02-2004 .

Although we have told you to pay the amount you owe, it is still not paid. This is your copy of a notice of levy we have sent to collect this unpaid amount. We will send other levies if we do not get enough with this one.

Banks, credit unions, savings and loans, and similar institutions described in Section 408(n) of the Internal Revenue Code **must hold your money for 21 calendar days** before sending it to us. They must include the interest you earn during that time. Anyone else we send a levy to must turn over your money, property, credits, etc. that they have (or are already obligated for) when they would have paid you.

If you decide to pay the amount you owe now, please **bring** a guaranteed payment (cash, cashier's check, certified check, or money order) to the nearest IRS office with form, so we can tell the person who received this levy not to send us your money. If you mail your payment instead of bringing it to us, we may not have time to stop the person who received this levy from sending us your money.

If we have erroneously levied your bank account, we may reimburse you for the fees your bank charged you for handling the levy. You must file a claim with the IRS on Form 8546 within one year after the fees are charged.

If you have any questions or want to arrange payment before other levies are issued, please call or write us. If you write to us, please include your telephone number and the best time to call.

Signature of Service Representative

Title **Operations Manager, Collection**

# <u>Caption</u>
# *EXHIBIT NO. 36*

October 22, 2004

I called a number listed for the Pittsburgh office. No one answers,
I am given a Fax number. They really don't like to talk to people.
No response to this letter. No response or acknowledgement is ever
received.

To: IRS Lien Dept.
            Director, Payment Compliance

From:

                         October 22,2004

Re:  Federal Tax Lien

   I called the number listed on the notice and was given this Fax number.

   May I offer a brief background, from my position, for this situation.  Approximately 4 months ago, your Philadelphia office called me and said that the statute of limitations would expire at the end of this year, and the agency wanted to resolve this issue.  I stated that I also wanted such action.  I was asked what amount of cash could be raised from liquid assets.  I told the gentleman, approximately $24,000.  He stated that the agency would want that money since a payment plan could not be initiated due the stated expiration date.  I was told to get Form 433, complete it, and take it to the Reading, PA. office.  I did that.  The person at the counter had no knowledge of my information.  She told me to leave the paperwork and I would get a response.

   Approximately 4 weeks later I get a hand written note telling me to close my savings, equity and IRA account and send the check to the local office. (Approx. $24,000).  She also said I should pay $1630/month for 40 months.  This is somewhat different than what I was told by Philadelphia.  How am I to know who is correct?  She also told me to submit new 443A/B forms, which I did.  She also sent me OIC and Payment Plan forms.

   I closed all these accounts, mailed a check, along with an explanation of my actions.  I never got a response, and the check was never cashed.  This was around early Oct.

   On Saturday, Oct 16, I received a certified letter informing me that I lien had been placed against my home.  On Monday, the 18th my bank called and said that my account was frozen, and on Tuesday my employer informed me that they received paperwork to begin the process to  levy against my wages.  There is more conflicting information on this matter, but  I know you have no interest.

   I am 67 years old.  I retired 2 yr. ago, but returned to work .  My employer is very upset with this garnishment.  It is very difficult to find employment at 67.  My  outlook for continued employment is very grim, and  may  be on layoff very shortly.  I have a brother who recently had a 5 way bypass and another going for a checkup due to similar findings.  My job is also very physical.  If medical problems, or an employment loss hit me, it is very unlikely that  further  employment will  be available to me.

I would like to ask a question. After the amount due per pay cycle is determined, can I pay direct without involving my employer? I also assume you will take the $27,000 frozen in my bank account and put it against this liability. Also, if I provide the difference between the bank amount and the amount of the lien on my home, will the lien be removed? I would also like to offer several options for your consideration.

First, I doubt very much that I will be working full time two years from this date. If my calculations are correct, the levy on my wages would require approximately 6 years of payment. There is no way I will we working at 70, let alone 73. When I stop working, what happens, whether it be for medical reasons, or simply that no one wants a 70 year old man?

1. I offer $750/mo. for 2 years in addition to the $27K you will take from my account. This assumes I can retain present employment and salary level.

2. I offer a lump sum payment of $15K sometime during the first quarter of 2005, in addition to the $27K. This amount will be obtained through a personal loan or a Home equity loan. The need for the lien to be removed from the home. I will also pay $750/month until the monies are available (1st Q 05). If not available I will continue to pay for 2 yrs as stated in No. 1.

At this point my main concern is the involvement of my employer. If I loose my job because of this, I have no more to offer. If you insist on the garnishment and reject both proposals, I ask that you allow me to pay directly.

# *Caption*
# *EXHIBIT NO. 37*

June 27, 2005

My Appeal is denied. I am told you can only appeal one time. Why do they continue to send me the Appeal form? I file a request to withdraw the Process Hearing and the OIC. Note the letter writer sets the statute of limitations at August 29,2007. My attorney tells me I will have wage garnishment for two more years.

Internal Revenue Service
Appeals Office

Department of the Treasury

Person to Contact:

Philadelphia, PA .

Employee ID Number:
Tel:
Fax:

Date: June 27, 2005

Refer Reply to:

In Re:
   Collection Due Process - Lien
Tax Period(s) Ended:
   03/1991

Dear Mr.

This is in reference to your request for a Collection Due Process hearing with regard to the lien and the offer in compromise that you submitted as your collection alternative. On Form 12153 you checked off both lien and levy. You had a prior hearing concerning the levy issue. As only one levy hearing for the same period is allowed, I will only address the lien issue.

You raise two issues in your request for a hearing: the underlying liability and the correctness of the collection statute.

The provisions of IRC 6330(c)(2)(B) are a statutory bar to contest the liability under Collection Due Process if you previously had the ability to do so. Our records show that you had protested the proposed assessment and Appeals sustained the decision to assess the Trust Fund Recovery Penalty. You cannot raise this issue again.

With regard to the collection statute, the original statute would have expired 12/5/2004, however the statute was extended both by your bankruptcy petition (7/8/1998-6/18/1999) and your earlier Collection Due Process hearing for the levy (9/6/2002-6/20/2004). The updated statute is 8/29/2007. The statute is further extended by this hearing and the submission of the offer, however they run concurrently.

I have reviewed your proposed offer and cannot recommend its acceptance. Doubt as to liability cannot be used in your case for a reason for the offer. A review of your financial information shows that the balance due can be paid off within the extended collection statute without creating a hardship.

If you want to stop the further extension of the collection statute, I suggest that you withdraw both the offer and the Collection Due Process hearing. I have enclosed Form 12257 and a letter of withdrawal for the offer for that purpose. The result will be that the levy will remain in place for the life of the statute, but no additional enforcement action will take place. The lien will not be released until the liability is paid in full or the statute tolls, whichever comes first.

-2-

Let me know how you want me to proceed in this matter by July 6, 2005.

Sincerely,

Settlement Officer

Enclosures:
 Envelope
 Form 12256; Offer Withdrawal Letter

## ...... .. .v.quest tor Collection Due Process Hearing

*(Please print the information in the spaces below.)*

Taxpayer Name(s):

Taxpayer address:

| City | State | Zip code |
|------|-------|----------|
|      |       |          |

Type of tax/Tax form number(s)*

Tax Period(s)*     03/1991

Social Security/Employer Identification Number(s)*

*(Note: *You may attach a copy of your* Collection Due Process *notice to this form instead of listing the tax type/form number/period and identification number in the spaces above.*)

I've reached a resolution with the Internal Revenue Service regarding the tax and tax periods that my hearing request concerned and I'm satisfied that I no longer need a hearing with Appeals. Therefore, I withdraw my request for a Collection Due Process (CDP) Hearing under:

X     Internal Revenue Code (IRC) Section 6320, notice and opportunity for a hearing upon the filing of a Notice of Federal Tax Lien

___     IRC Section 6330, notice and opportunity for a hearing before a levy

___     Both IRC Section 6320 and 6330

**understand that by withdrawing my request:**

- I give up my right to a Collection Due Process Hearing with the Office of Appeals. I understand that the Office of Appeals will not issue a Notice of Determination with respect to the tax and tax periods the hearing request concerned.

- I give up my right to seek judicial review, in the Tax Court or a U.S. District Court, of the Notice of Determination that the Office of Appeals would have issued as a result of the Collection Due Process Hearing, as the Office of Appeals will not issue a Notice of Determination.

- I give up my right to have the Office of Appeals retain jurisdiction with respect to any determination that it would have made as a result of the Collection Due Process Hearing.

- The suspension of levy action and the suspension of the statute of limitations on the period of collection, as required under the provisions of IRC Sections 6320, are no longer in effect upon the receipt by Internal Revenue Service (IRS) of this withdrawal.

- I have the right to request a hearing with the Office of Appeals that is equivalent to a Collection Due Process Hearing without judicial appeal to the Tax Court or a U.S. District Court under IRC Section 6320 or 6330.

   I do not give up any other appeal rights that I am entitled to, such as an appeal under the Collection Appeals Program (CAP).

r's signature

Spouse's signature (if applicable)

zed representative's signature (if applicable)

For privacy Act information please refer to Notice 609

nt of the Treasury - Internal Revenue Service          www.irs.gov          Form 12256-c (Rev. 6/1999)

I wish to withdraw my offer in compromise dated 1/10/2005.

7/18/05

Date

# Caption
# *EXHIBIT NO. 38*

August 30, 2005

One letter acknowledges my request for withdrawal of Request for Hearing. The other letter acknowledges withdrawal of the OIC.

Internal Revenue Service
Appeals Office

Philadelphia, PA

Date: *August 30, 2005*

Department of the Treasury

**Person to Contact:**

  Employee ID Number:
  Tel:
  Fax:
**Refer Reply to:**

**In Re:**
  Offer in Compromise
**Tax Period(s) Ended:**
  03/1991

Dear Mr. .

This refers to your offer of $9,000.00, submitted to compromise your liability for the period(s) shown above.

The offer is considered withdrawn as of July 21, 2005.

In your letter of July 18, 2005 you state in part:

"I wish to withdraw my offer in compromise dated 1/10/2005."

If you have not already done so, please contact the Collection Division about settlement of your account.

Thank you for your cooperation.

                        Sincerely,

                        Appeals Team Manager

ᴵᶜ ᴵᴵᴵ ⁰¹ ⁻ᵐ 10 46

I wish to withdraw my offer in compromise dated 1/10/2005.

7/18/05
Date

**Internal Revenue Service**
Appeals Office

Philadelphia, PA

Date: *August 30, 2005*

**Department of the Treasury**

**Person to Contact:**

Employee ID Number:
Tel:
Fax:
**Refer Reply to:**

**In Re:**
Collection Due Process - Lien
**Tax Period(s) Ended:**
03/1991

Dear Mr.

This is to acknowledge receipt of your Form 12256, Withdrawal of Request for Collection Due Process Hearing.

If you have any questions, please contact the person whose name and telephone number are shown above.

Sincerely,

Appeals Team Manager

## Withdrawal of Request for Collection Due Process Hearing

*(Please print the information in the spaces below.)*

axpayer Name(s):

axpayer address:

| itv | State | Zip code |
|-----|-------|----------|
|     |       |          |

ype of tax/Tax form number(s)*

ax Period(s)*    03/1991

ocial Security/Employer Identification Number(s)*

*(Note: *You may attach a copy of your Collection Due Process notice to this form instead of listing the tax type/form number/period and* identification number in the spaces above.)

e reached a resolution with the Internal Revenue Service regarding the tax and tax periods that my hearing request concerned and I'm satisfied that I no nger need a hearing with Appeals. Therefore, I withdraw my request for a Collection Due Process (CDP) Hearing under:

K_ Internal Revenue Code (IRC) Section 6320, notice and opportunity for a hearing upon the filing of a Notice of Federal Tax Lien

___ IRC Section 6330, notice and opportunity for a hearing before a levy

___ Both IRC Section 6320 and 6330

understand that by withdrawing my request:

* I give up my right to a Collection Due Process Hearing with the Office of Appeals. I understand that the Office of Appeals will not issue a Notice of Determination with respect to the tax and tax periods the hearing request concerned.

* I give up my right to seek judicial review, in the Tax Court or a U.S. District Court, of the Notice of Determination that the Office of Appeals would have issued as a result of the Collection Due Process Hearing, as the Office of Appeals will not issue a Notice of Determination.

* I give up my right to have the Office of Appeals retain jurisdiction with respect to any determination that it would have made as a result of the Collection Due Process Hearing.

* The suspension of levy action and the suspension of the statute of limitations on the period of collection, as required under the provisions of IRC Sections 6320, are no longer in effect upon the receipt by Internal Revenue Service (IRS) of this withdrawal.

* I have the right to request a hearing with the Office of Appeals that is equivalent to a Collection Due Process Hearing without judicial appeal to the Tax Court or a U.S. District Court under IRC Section 6320 or 6330.

* I do not give up any other appeal rights that I am entitled to, such as an appeal under the Collection Appeals Program (CAP).

payer's signature                                  Spouse's signature *(if applicable)*

horized representative's signature *(if applicable)*

For privacy Act information please refer to Notice 609

rtment of the Treasury - Internal Revenue Service          www.irs.gov          Form 12256-c (Rev. 6/1999)

<u>_Caption_</u>

# _EXHIBIT NO. 39_

September 26, 2005

Pay up, or we will proceed with levy action to take 15% of your social security benefits.

 **IRS** Department of the Treasury
Internal Revenue Service
KANSAS CITY, MO

Notice Number: CP
Notice Date: SEP. 26, 2005
Social Security Number:

| Collection Assistance: |
| --- |
| *(Asistencia en español disponible)* |
| Caller ID: |

### Final Notice Before Levy On Social Security Benefits

Our records indicate the federal tax you owe has not been paid, although we have previously advised you of your appeal rights and asked you to pay it. The law allows the IRS to take up to 15% of your Social Security benefits to pay your overdue taxes. **We will proceed with levy action** if you do not pay the full amount you owe, request an appeals hearing, or contact us to resolve the tax matter within 30 days from the date of this notice.

We have identified the following Social Security account information:

> **Social Security Claim Account Number:**
> **Beneficiary's Own Account Number:**

To avoid this levy action against your Social Security benefits:

**If You Can Pay The Amount You Owe In Full:**
- Make your check or money order payable to the United States Treasury.
- Write your Social Security Number, the form number(s), and tax period(s) on your payment.
- Send your payment and the attached payment stub to us in the enclosed envelope.

You will find the amount you owe listed on the next page. The amount you owe includes tax, penalties, and interest. Penalty and interest charges, known as statutory additions, are detailed on the following pages and continue to accrue until you pay the total amount in full.

**If You Cannot Pay The Amount You Owe In Full:**
It is important that you call us immediately at the telephone number listed above. Please be prepared to tell us your monthly income and expenses so we can help you resolve this tax matter. We may be able to set up a payment arrangement. Or, if we determine that you cannot pay any of your tax debt due to a significant hardship, we may temporarily delay collection until your financial condition improves.

**Contact Us (Within 30 days from the date of this notice)**
Please do not contact the Social Security Administration regarding your federal tax matter. If you have any questions, please call the IRS at the above telephone number or write to us at the address located on the return stub found on the second page of this notice. We want to help you resolve this matter, so please call us if you need assistance.

**Authorized Representative**
If you wish to have someone else contact us to resolve this tax matter, complete Form 2848, *Power of Attorney and Declaration of Representative*, and send it to us in the enclosed envelope. You can get this form at your local IRS office, by calling 1-800-829-3676, or from our website at www.irs.gov. For your information, we have enclosed Publication 4134. This publication provides a list of Low Income Taxpayer Clinics that assist low-income taxpayers for free or for a nominal charge.

Enclosures:
Publication 4134
Copy of this notice
Envelope

CP 91 (Rev. 06-2005)

## <u>Caption</u>
## *EXHIBIT NO. 40*

Oct. 13, 2005

Hopefully, this is the last notice relative to the ending of the statute of limitations. This note states, 'November 7, 2008'. That's a long time away for me.
I really don't believe this is the final piece of correspondence relative to this matter. History says I am probably right.

# Internal Revenue Service

Campus Appeals

Department of the Treasury

Person to Contact:

Contact Telephone Number:

Hours Available: 8:00am-3:30pm PST
In Re: Civil Penalty
Tax Period Ending: March 1991

Date: Oct 13, 2005

Taxpayer Identification Number:

Dear Mr.

This letter serves as a follow up to our phone conversation of September 29, 2005. As I stated, the levy against you Social Security benefits was stopped. The continuous levy of      bi-weekly will stay in place.

The collection statute on the above account expires on November 7, 2008. The original statute would have expired on December 5, 2004 but was extended due to your bankruptcy petition (7/8/1998-6/18/1999), previous Collection Due Process hearing for the first levy (9/6/2002-6/20/2004), the current Collection Due Process hearing (11/08/2004-07/18/2005), and the Offer In Compromise (1/20/2005-7/18/2005).

If you have any questions, please contact me at the telephone number shown above for discussion. Thank you for your cooperation.

Sincerely yours,

Campus Appeals
Accounts Resolution Specialist

978-0-595-38752-6
0-595-38752-7